LARRY SANG'S

CHINESE ASTROLOGY & FENG SHUI GUIDE

2011

The Year of The Rabbit

with Lorraine Wilcox

LARRY SANG'S

The Year of the Rabbit

ASTROLOGY AND FENG SHUI GUIDE

Original Title:
Master Larry Sang's 2011 The Year of the Rabbit, Astrology and Feng Shui Guide

Published by: The American Feng Shui Institute
111 N. Atlantic Blvd, Suite 352
Monterey Park, CA 91754. U.S.A.
Email: fsinfo@amfengshui.com
www.amfengshui.com

Written by:
Master Larry Sang

Edited by:
Lorraine Wilcox

Cover Design & Illustration by:
Afriany Simbolon

*True faith and courage are like
a kite:
An opposing wind raises it
higher*

Calligraphy by Larry Sang

Please Read This Information

This book provides information regarding the subject matter covered. The authors are not engaged in rendering legal, medical or other professional advice. If you need medical or legal advice, a competent professional should be contacted. Chinese Astrology and Feng Shui are not get-rich-quick or cure-all schemes. Changes in your life will happen as fast as you are ready for them. Be patient in your study of Chinese Astrology and Feng Shui.

The authors have tried to make this book as complete and accurate as possible. However, there may be typographical or content mistakes. Use this book as a general guide in your study of Chinese Astrology and Feng Shui

This book was written to educate and entertain. The authors, distributors and the American Feng Shui Institute shall have neither liability nor responsibility to any person with respect to any loss or damage caused, or alleged to be caused by this book.

The following pages of predictions will help you understand trends as they develop through the coming year. Please keep in mind that they are somewhat general because other stellar influences are operative, according to the month, date and exact minute of your birth. Unfortunately, we cannot deal with each person individually in this book.

Table of Contents

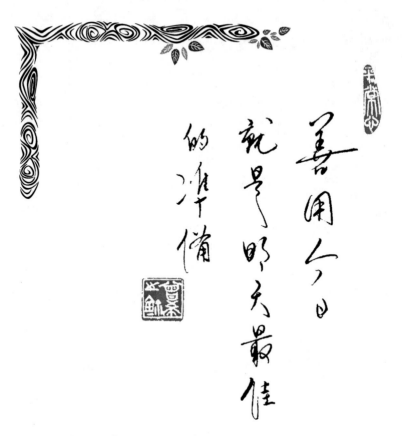

善用今日
就是明天最佳
的準備

The only preparation
for tomorrow is the
right use of today

How to find your Animal Sign

In order to find your correct animal sign, as well as understand why the Chinese calendar begins in February, and not January, it is important to have a little understanding of the two different Chinese calendars. As with most things Chinese, we look at the Yin and Yang. In Chinese timekeeping, there is a Yin calendar (lunar calendar) and a Yang calendar (solar calendar).

The Lunar Calendar

The Lunar Calendar is perhaps the best known and most popular of the two. Chinese Lunar New Year is frequently celebrated with a lot of pageantry. It is used in one type of Chinese astrology called Zi Wei Dou Shu, and also in Yi-Jing calculations.

The Solar Calendar

The Solar calendar is less well known. The early Chinese meteorologists attempted to gain insight into the cycles of the seasons. From this study, they developed the Solar calendar. This calendar is used in the form of Chinese Astrology called Four Pillars, as well as in Feng Shui. The Chinese were very accurate in their studies. Without computers, and using only observations, they mapped a solar year of 365 days. They missed the actual timing of a year by only 14 minutes and 12 seconds.

The solar year is divided into 24 solar terms. Each lasts about fifteen days. Spring Begins (lichun) is the name of the first day of spring, and the first solar term. It is exactly midway between the winter solstice and the spring equinox. This is why it always falls on February 4th or 5th. We begin the five elements with wood, so the Chinese New Year begins with a wood month, whether in the Lunar or the Solar calendar. These concepts are derived from the Yi-Jing.

How to find your Animal Sign

To find your animal sign, start with your birth date. If it is before February 4th (Spring Begins), use the prior year for the Chinese calendar. If it is after February 4th, then use the same birth year. If it is on February 4th, then you need the time of the birth to accurately determine the birth animal. This information is contained in the Chinese Ten-Thousand Year Calendar. (The American Feng Shui Institute has one available as an ebook at www.amfengshui.com). In the following pages, the birth years are listed for each animal, but remember, if your birthday is before February 4th, use the previous year to determine the animal.

The Twelve Animals

Rat 鼠	*Ox* 牛	*Tiger* 虎	*Rabbit* 兔
1924, 1936, 1948, 1960, 1972, 1984, 1996, 2008	1925, 1937, 1949, 1961, 1973, 1985, 1997, 2009	1926, 1938, 1950, 1962, 1974, 1986, 1998, 2010	1927, 1939, 1951, 1963, 1975, 1987, 1999, 2011
Dragon 龍	*Snake* 蛇	*Horse* 馬	*Sheep* 羊
1928, 1940, 1952, 1964, 1976, 1988, 2000	1929, 1941, 1953, 1965, 1977, 1989, 2001	1930, 1942, 1954, 1966, 1978, 1990, 2002	1931, 1943, 1955, 1967, 1979, 1991, 2003
Monkey 猴	*Rooster* 雞	*Dog* 狗	*Pig* 豬
1932, 1944, 1956, 1968, 1980, 1992, 2004	1933, 1945, 1957, 1969, 1981, 1993, 2005	1934, 1946, 1958, 1970, 1982, 1994, 2006	1935, 1947, 1959, 1971, 1983, 1995, 2007

Fortunes of the 12 Animals

The Rabbit

1927, 1939, 1951, 1963, 1975, 1987, 1999, 2011

Note: The New Year begins February 4th

2011 is a year of abundant opportunities for the Rabbit. In career, the best strategy is to cultivate flexibility. The Rabbit's character may prefer security and stability to uncertainty and change, but this year you need to embrace the unknown to achieve your potential. You can achieve success if you venture abroad, whether it is for studies or emigration. Career and money prospects are at their best during the summer and autumn. At times, especially during the 8th Chinese month, lucrative opportunities should present themselves, but guard against greed. Don't push your luck on risky investments. Money luck is extremely strong for Rabbits born in 1951. Relaxation is valuable to your health this year. The Rabbit has a tendency to never fully unwind, even when participating in so-called leisure activities. Therefore, it is in your best interest to ensure you get enough sleep, and to practice healthy exercise and nutrition so your body can recover from overindulgence. Where romance is concerned, lovers and spouses tend to be temperamental, so frequent squabbles may take place. To prevent a break up, you must control your temper and think twice before you act.

Your Benefactor is: Tiger
(1926, 1938, 1950, 1962, 1974, 1986, 1998, 2010)

12 Month Outlook For The Rabbit

Solar Month	Comments
1st Month Feb 4th - Mar 5th	A rewarding month. Most things are to your satisfaction.
2nd Month Mar 6th - Apr 4th	Take care of your physical health. Be cautious of minor cuts.
3rd Month Apr 5th - May 5th	You may be in low spirits. Beneficial for venturing overseas.
4th Month May 6th - June 5th	An auspicious month. Career will be smooth sailing.
5th Month June 6th - July 6th	This is a good time to plan or to learn something new.
6th Month July 7th - Aug 7th	Things may suddenly turn sour. Be cautious of conflicts in relationships.
7th Month Aug 8th - Sept 7th	Career luck is in good view. Things come out well.
8th Month Sept 8th - Oct 7th	Money luck is strong. Money could flow in from unanticipated sources.
9th Month Oct 8th - Nov 7th	Don't expect too much. Be tolerant. You are prone to get angry over trivial matters.
10th Month Nov 8th - Dec 6th	A very auspicious time to offer or receive a marriage proposal!
11th Month Dec 7th - Jan 5th	Though there is pressure on your job, money and career are in good view.
12th Month Jan 6th - Feb 3rd	Things will be relatively peaceful.

The Dragon

1928, 1940, 1952, 1964, 1976, 1988, 2000

Note: The New Year begins February 4th

The Rabbit year brings good tidings to the Dragon. Good news can be expected within the family. In career, the Dragon's natural leadership and charisma are enhanced, and you may find your ideas and initiatives get more traction than usual. This year will present opportunities of your wildest imaginings, but you will need abundant self-discipline in order to make them reality. Success is within your reach, but beware of pride and overconfidence; it is not a foregone conclusion. Though money prospects are average to good, your expenditures will rise correspondingly. You should be a bit careful with your health. If you find yourself overworked, take a step back and focus on meditation or a soothing exercise such as Yoga. Remember, stress tends to cause an increase in stomach acid so it is wise for you to avoid too many fried foods and caffeine. Common complaints this year are mental stress, digestion, and minor cuts. Where romance is concerned, married Dragons will enjoy productive relationships with peers and family members. The single Dragon will have no trouble finding a prospective spouse, but, it is better for you to take the initiative. This is especially true with single Dragons born in 1988. However, Dragon lovers and couples should be wary of the intrusion of a third party.

Your Benefactor is: Rabbit
(1927, 1939, 1951, 1963, 1975, 1987, 1999, 2011)

12 Month Outlook For The Dragon

Solar Month	Comments
1st Month Feb 4th - Mar 5th	Average luck. Pay attention to your health to avoid minor illness or cuts.
2nd Month Mar 6th - Apr 4th	This is a relatively favorable month for travel, but exercise caution and heed your hunches.
3rd Month Apr 5th - May 5th	Strong Peach Blossom. This is a joyous time for females but complicated relationships for males.
4th Month May 6th - June 5th	Luck is steady and smooth.
5th Month June 6th - July 6th	You can easily feel depressed and moody.
6th Month July 7th - Aug 7th	Money luck is "easy come easy go."
7th Month Aug 8th - Sept 7th	Beneficial to develop something new. Salaried workers can expect a promotion.
8th Month Sept 8th - Oct 7th	Be cautious of gossip. Lots of confusion in dealing with things.
9th Month Oct 8th - Nov 7th	Auspicious stars Tian De and Fu Xing shine above! Good in all aspects.
10th Month Nov 8th - Dec 6th	This is a rather auspicious month. You will be quite busy.
11th Month Dec 7th - Jan 5th	Everything you do will be almost effortless.
12th Month Jan 6th - Feb 3rd	There are signs of unexpected gain and a benefactor coming forward.

The Snake

1929, 1941, 1953, 1965, 1977, 1989, 2001

Note: The New Year begins February 4ᵗʰ

In 2011, the Snake's career and money luck alternate between good and bad. Change can be uncomfortable for the Snake, but if you recognize that the transformations can ultimately be in your favor, adapting will be easier. There may be only a few opportunities, but stay alert and be ready to take full advantage so you can make them count. In the meantime, direct your energy to areas in which you have the most expertise. The Snake's natural tendency is to be independent and trust your own judgment above all. However, giving added weight to the advice and wisdom of others in this Rabbit year could prove extremely worthwhile. Be diplomatic; you can't afford personal conflict on the job. Health-wise, rapid change and uncertainty can take its toll on the Snake's nerves in 2011. You may feel pressure to abandon enjoyable leisure activities to meet many stressful demands, but this would be a mistake. It is important for you to attend carefully to both your physical and mental health. Expectant mothers should take extra care to prevent miscarriage. Where romance is concerned, married Snakes may find themselves neglected. For the single Snakes, it is likely to be smooth and joyful. It is a favorable time for you to put yourself into new environments and social circles. You should be well-received, but you need to make the first move.

Your Benefactor is: Snake
(1929, 1941, 1953, 1965, 1977, 1989, 2001)

12 Month Outlook For The Snake

Solar Month	Comments
1st Month Feb 4th - Mar 5th	A very auspicious time for you to do business abroad or with foreign companies.
2nd Month Mar 6th - Apr 4th	There are signs of unexpected gain and a benefactor coming forward.
3rd Month Apr 5th - May 5th	Luck is average to good. There are big gains and small losses.
4th Month May 6th - June 5th	Good for venturing overseas.
5th Month June 6th - July 6th	Money luck is strong. Things are average to good.
6th Month July 7th - Aug 7th	Auspicious stars shine above, things are smooth and enjoyable
7th Month Aug 8th - Sept 7th	You are likely to incur unnecessary expenditures. Be on your guard, keep expenses under control.
8th Month Sept 8th - Oct 7th	There are signs of an unexpected benefactor showing up. A good opportunity comes your way.
9th Month Oct 8th - Nov 7th	Conditions stimulate you to try something different.
10th Month Nov 8th - Dec 6th	Be conservative. Be alert for signs of overspending.
11th Month Dec 7th - Jan 5th	Stay flexible throughout the month. Carefully look for the jade among the trash.
12th Month Jan 6th - Feb 3rd	A busy month. Do not go too fast. Slow down and double check all documents before you sign.

The Horse

1918, 1930, 1942, 1954, 1966, 1978, 1990, 2002

Note: The New Year begins February 4th

Auspicious stars shining above will bring wealth and fame for the Horse in 2011. Career and money prospects are most promising. Expanding your business or getting a promotion is easy if the Horse proceeds in a bold, but cautious manner. There are signs of unexpected gains and benefactors. But stiff competition lies ahead for you and makes you feel a lot of pressure in work. The self-employed will have more opportunities for further development. With hard work, you will bring about substantial gain. Those who were born in 1978 may have unexpected good news coming their way. Health-wise, burnout is a risk this year, avoid excessive work. For your mental health, it's advisable to take up some hobby or interest that is completely new to you and that doesn't directly relate to your current goals or responsibilities. The path to romance is featured prominently in this Rabbit year. For the single Horse, attend as many events and gatherings as possible, or better yet, plan some yourself. Expanding your social circle and interests will connect you with exciting new love prospects. Married couples should avoid dwelling too much on past relationships.

Your Benefactor is: Ox
(1925, 1937, 1949, 1961, 1973, 1985, 1997, 2009)

12 Month Outlook For The Horse

Solar Month	Comments
1st Month Feb 4th - Mar 5th	Auspicious stars shine above! Good fortune goes hand in hand with you and puts you in the right time, right place.
2nd Month Mar 6th - Apr 4th	Luck is smooth, daily activities and surroundings are easier to handle than usual.
3rd Month Apr 5th - May 5th	Be alert for signs of discomfort due to stress.
4th Month May 6th - June 5th	Auspicious money luck. For salaried-workers, there is a future promotion or pay raise.
5th Month June 6th - July 6th	Good luck. Plot future plans with care; the benefits will be everything you could hope for.
6th Month July 7th - Aug 7th	Be conservative. Signs of conflict.
7th Month Aug 8th - Sept 7th	This is a relatively favorable month for travel. Sign of strong peach blossom.
8th Month Sept 8th - Oct 7th	A month of mixed good and bad. Avoid being arrogant.
9th Month Oct 8th - Nov 7th	An unexpected benefactor may come forward. Accept offers without reservation.
10th Month Nov 8th - Dec 6th	Do all that you can to boost business prospects. Things will come out well.
11th Month Dec 7th - Jan 5th	Keep on high alert. A sign of relationship breakup or cuts.
12th Month Jan 6th - Feb 3rd	A new opportunity waiting for you. Beneficial to travel.

The Sheep

1931, 1943, 1955, 1967, 1979, 1991, 2003

Note: The New Year begins February 4th

This is a moderate year for the Sheep with neither signs of danger nor major breakthroughs. Your favorable times are the 6th, 9th, and 12th Chinese months. Business affairs should speed along. Those are the best months of the year to discuss new plans or launch a campaign. Advertising and public relations are vital to success. Make full use of these months to work hard and fight for what you want. As for the 2nd, 4th, and 5th months, things do not look so good; things may go quite wrong because there are hidden dangers. Put a hold on new proposals until current work nears completion. It is all too easy to overextend yourself and wind up with a less than satisfactory results. So be careful and do not attempt to dodge responsibility because of an error in judgment. Money luck is average; your cautious approach will serve you well in 2010. Health is fine. You may have occasional minor discomforts, but no major problems. Sheep born in 1955 and 1979 who love alcohol should be cautious of making a big mistake due to of their drinking. Romance is average to good. If it comes, let it come, and if it goes, let it go. Do not force the issue. Those who are married may find their spouses are emotionally distant and have difficulty communicating with each other. Be wary of a third party intrusion.

Your Benefactor is: Rat
(1924, 1936, 1948, 1960, 1972, 1984, 1996, 2008)

12 Month Outlook For The Sheep

Solar Month	Comments
1st Month Feb 4th - Mar 5th	This is not the time to be creative or try something new.
2nd Month Mar 6th - Apr 4th	Some obstacles lie ahead. Don't retain high expectations or be greedy about money matters beyond your capability.
3rd Month Apr 5th - May 5th	Average luck. Relying on your own efforts is the best approach.
4th Month May 6th - June 5th	Put off any uncertain projects until you are sure you have examined all the angles.
5th Month June 6th - July 6th	Do not trust anything sight unseen, otherwise you may find yourself in an embarrassing situation.
6th Month July 7th - Aug 7th	This is a good month for career and money luck.
7th Month Aug 8th - Sept 7th	Things are not as clear as they seemed last month. Hold a wait-and-see attitude until the situation clarifies.
8th Month Sept 8th - Oct 7th	Do not rush in affairs. Your mental processes are not as good as usual.
9th Month Oct 8th - Nov 7th	Though there is pressure on your job, money and career are in good view.
10th Month Nov 8th - Dec 6th	Be careful to avoid cuts and minor health problems.
11th Month Dec 7th - Jan 5th	Be on guard. It is likely to incur unnecessary expenditures.
12th Month Jan 6th - Feb 3rd	Auspicious luck. You can get almost everything you want.

The Monkey

Note: The New Year begins February 4th

The Monkey's luck in 2011 is inconsistent. Obstacles will stand in the way of your career. Proceed a little more cautiously as the Tiger year draws to a close and the Rabbit year begins. However, things will improve by late July, and good luck is on your side in the end. In career, beware of being cheated or sold out by others. Don't allow negativism to affect your own outlook. Keep all moves simple and straightforward so that no one can accuse you of deception. Money prospects alternate between good and bad during spring and summer. To prevent financial losses, avoid lending money or acting as guarantors for others in March. Promises that were made during spring and summer are not reliable. A supporter you have been counting on may back off in June. There is little chance of obtaining a loan or other financial backing before the end of July. In health, watch out for illnesses of the digestive system. Avoid overworking and abstain from liquor. Where romance is concerned, the single Monkey will find this a relatively uneventful year because of things beyond your control. You should not mistake friendliness for love. Married couples should refrain from quarreling over trivial matters which may lead to separation.

Your Benefactor is: Pig
(1923, 1935, 1947, 1959, 1971, 1983, 1995, 2007)

12 Month Outlook For The Monkey	
Solar Month	**Comments**
1st Month Feb 4th - Mar 5th	Proceed with things cautiously, unbeneficial for developing something new.
2nd Month Mar 6th - Apr 4th	Money prospects are good.
3rd Month Apr 5th - May 5th	There are signs of unexpected gains and you may discover a new source of income.
4th Month May 6th - June 5th	Travel can put you in contact with a person who will benefit your career in the future.
5th Month June 6th - July 6th	Things you do will be almost effortless.
6th Month July 7th - Aug 7th	This is a rather auspicious month. Career will be smooth sailing.
7th Month Aug 8th - Sept 7th	You will be quite busy. Luck is moving forward.
8th Month Sept 8th - Oct 7th	Auspicious luck. A stroke of luck may put you in position for a special assignment.
9th Month Oct 8th - Nov 7th	Conflict arises easily. Be cautious in your speech and think before taking action.
10th Month Nov 8th - Dec 6th	Things may suddenly turn sour. Be cautious of money loss.
11th Month Dec 7th - Jan 5th	Auspicious stars shine above! All work is mostly highly rewarded.
12th Month Jan 6th - Feb 3rd	Good in all aspects. You are busy and march forward smoothly.

The Rooster

1921, 1933, 1945, 1957, 1969, 1981, 1993, 2005

Note: The New Year begins February 4th

Since 2011 is the Po Sui year for the Rooster, it will be an unstable time of floating and sinking. The Rooster's fortune this year is ever-changing. Don't expect windfalls, avoid gambling or indulging in financial speculation. The self-employed can expand their business; a profitable investment opportunity will come your way in August or September. Salaried workers may find themselves facing a lot of pressure, particularly Roosters born in 1969. But as long as you work hard, promotion and a raise in pay are easily yours. The strong star of money-luck, Lu Cun, mixes together with the Big Consuming star; this makes the Rooster's money come in substantially and flow back out too. Avoid visiting the sick or attending funerals to guard against receiving bad luck in the form of illness or money loss. Health-wise, there are no life-threatening illnesses. Common health complaints for the Rooster are painful joints, rheumatism, and so forth. Romance for the single Rooster comes and goes; the one you love may not turn out to be as sincere as you think. For married couples, your loved one may run hot and cold. An extraordinary relationship will come your way if you free your mind.

Your Benefactor is: Rooster
(1933, 1945, 1957, 1969, 1981, 1993, 2005)

12 Month Outlook For The Rooster

Solar Month	Comments
1st Month Feb 4th - Mar 5th	This month can bring conflict and tension. Try to avoid people who aggravate you.
2nd Month Mar 6th - Apr 4th	A good opportunity is awaiting you. Fight hard for what you want.
3rd Month Apr 5th - May 5th	Be conservative and go step by step.
4th Month May 6th - June 5th	Be ready to take advantage of a change this month. Good opportunity.
5th Month June 6th - July 6th	Auspicious luck! Things are pleasurable. Money luck is strong.
6th Month July 7th - Aug 7th	Average luck. You feel busy physically and mentally.
7th Month Aug 8th - Sept 7th	Luck is strong. An auspicious time for you to plan something new or switch jobs.
8th Month Sept 8th - Oct 7th	Be tolerant. Luck is mixed between good and bad.
9th Month Oct 8th - Nov 7th	Steady and smooth. Keep working hard and mind your own business.
10th Month Nov 8th - Dec 6th	Money and career have good signs, but try to prevent over-spending for no reason.
11th Month Dec 7th - Jan 5th	Auspicious luck! Things are pleasurable. Money luck is strong.
12th Month Jan 6th - Feb 3rd	Take care of elderly family members. Be cautious with your own health as well.

The Dog

1922, 1934, 1946, 1958, 1970, 1982, 1994, 2006

Note: The New Year begins February 4th

The Dog will sail through the Rabbit year without any hitches. Your year has arrived, and you are likely to find it more comfortable than most. A career switch brings about good results. Career and money prospects are particularly rewarding. Good luck coupled with hard work will bring about substantial gains. The Dog's natural loyalty and charisma are enhanced this year, and you may find your ideas and initiatives get more traction than usual. Working people have prospects for venturing overseas, and good academic results come to those still in school. Travel can put you in contact with a person who benefits your career in the future. An invitation to join in a business venture will be forthcoming. If you intend to go into a partnership, it is best approach people born in the Sheep or Horse year. This year will present opportunities of your wildest imaginings, but you need abundant self-discipline in order to make them reality. Success is within your reach, but beware of pride and overconfidence; it is not a foregone conclusion. Health-wise, there are signs that the Dog over-works this year. Take preventive measures against chronic illness caused by stress. Where romance is concerned, a fruitful relationship will come your way. This year you may find a suitable life partner.

Your Benefactor is: Sheep
(1919, 1931, 1943, 1955, 1967, 1979, 1991, 2003)

12 Month Outlook For The Dog

Solar Month	Comments
1st Month Feb 4th - Mar 5th	Lots of good opportunities come your way.
2nd Month Mar 6th - Apr 4th	Be satisfied with small gains – don't expect too much.
3rd Month Apr 5th - May 5th	Auspicious stars shine above! This is a good month for courting couples to get married.
4th Month May 6th - June 5th	Be cautious. Do not go out late at night. It is easy to receive an injury.
5th Month June 6th - July 6th	Things are frustrating and rough. Dealing humbly with others will soften the situation.
6th Month July 7th - Aug 7th	Good luck. You will receive some unexpected benefit from your hard work.
7th Month Aug 8th - Sept 7th	Things are average to good, but it will be easy to arouse gossip and misunderstanding.
8th Month Sept 8th - Oct 7th	Beneficial to travel. You will have new opportunities.
9th Month Oct 8th - Nov 7th	A rewarding month. You can get almost everything you expect.
10th Month Nov 8th - Dec 6th	Beneficial luck for social relationships.
11th Month Dec 7th - Jan 5th	You may frequently feel unwell or moody.
12th Month Jan 6th - Feb 3rd	Money prospects are at their best for females. Life is average for males.

The Pig

1923, 1935, 1947, 1959, 1971, 1983, 1995, 2007

Note: The New Year begins February 4th

Pigs are likely to face challenges in 2011. The Rabbit year may not be an easy year for the Pig. But don't be depressed, this Rabbit year will provide Pigs with more opportunities. It is a near certainty that 2011 will bring Pigs at least one dramatic change in their career, whether a new role in your position or a different job altogether. Whether this change is voluntary or discouraging, you should take heart that these transitions hold a wealth of potential for you. Even if your new job isn't what you expect, or is somewhat disappointing, it will some day lead to more desirable opportunities you couldn't have anticipated. Do your best in any situation and you will receive ample recognition next year for the dues you pay now. Money luck is climbing up, and there are signs that unexpected side-money comes your way in September. Overall health is not foreseen as a problem area for Pigs during 2011. Avoid stress brought on by over-work. Watch out for illness caused by fatigue. Where romance is concerned, this is quite an uneventful year for romance. Single Pigs may give little thought to romance early in the year as other matters predominate. Marriage should wait as this is not a good year to tie the knot. Pigs born in 1960 should watch out for signs of their spouses' infidelity.

Your Benefactor is: Monkey
(1920, 1932, 1944, 1956, 1968, 1980, 1992, 2004)

12 Month Outlook For The Pig

Solar Month	Comments
1st Month Feb 4th - Mar 5th	Be conservative. It is easy to arouse gossip and misunderstanding
2nd Month Mar 6th - Apr 4th	Auspicious luck. A stroke of luck may put you in position for a special assignment.
3rd Month Apr 5th - May 5th	Things are steadily going up.
4th Month May 6th - June 5th	Take care of elderly family members. Be cautious with your own health as well.
5th Month June 6th - July 6th	Money luck is strong! You will feel great. Most of your work is highly rewarded.
6th Month July 7th - Aug 7th	You may be in a low mood. Luck is mixed. Don't expect too much.
7th Month Aug 8th - Sept 7th	Luck is average. Be careful about over-spending.
8th Month Sept 8th - Oct 7th	Auspicious luck. Career and money prospects are rewarding.
9th Month Oct 8th - Nov 7th	A rewarding month. You can get almost everything you expect.
10th Month Nov 8th - Dec 6th	Average luck. Regarding money, trust no one.
11th Month Dec 7th - Jan 5th	Watch out for cash-flow problems and budget wisely.
12th Month Jan 6th - Feb 3rd	Everything is smooth and enjoyable.

The Rat

1924, 1936, 1948, 1960, 1972, 1984, 1996, 2008

Note: The New Year begins February 4th

It will be a smooth sailing year for the Rat with good prospects in career and finance. However, 2011 can unnerve the Rat, especially after what have likely been two years of steady progress. This year could present great long-term opportunities in the Rat's profession, but you may not readily see it unless you are willing to reconsider well-laid plans. It is not a good time to push ahead too boldly. Rather, focus on maintaining gains already made and strengthening your professional reputation. Better yet, make yourself more valuable in your field by diversifying your skills and pursuing additional accreditations or qualifications; this will be fruitful this year. Money prospects are good and there may be lucrative opportunities where wealth is concerned, so you should investigate and take advantage of them. But, your expenditures will rise correspondingly. Rats could suffer the effects of exhaustion this year without even realizing they have overexerted themselves. Take extra precautions to ensure you get enough sleep, and practice healthy exercise to allow your body to recover from overindulgences. Where romance is concerned, because the Hong Luan Star shines above, a fruitful relationship will come your way. This is a good year for courting couples to get married.

Your Benefactor is: Dragon
(1928, 1940, 1952, 1964, 1976, 1988, 2000)

12 Month Outlook For The Rat

Solar Month	Comments
1st Month Feb 4th - Mar 5th	Auspicious luck. Strong peach blossom energy (romance and social relationships) around you.
2nd Month Mar 6th - Apr 4th	Things are average to good, but it will be easy to arouse gossip.
3rd Month Apr 5th - May 5th	Luck is low. To be safe, pay more attention to your health and do not visit sick people.
4th Month May 6th - June 5th	Money luck is strong! All work is highly rewarded.
5th Month June 6th - July 6th	Luck is mixed. Relaxation is the top priority.
6th Month July 7th - Aug 7th	You may frequently feel unwell or moody.
7th Month Aug 8th - Sept 7th	Career and money prospects are good. Focus on your target and work hard; the results will be what you planned.
8th Month Sept 8th - Oct 7th	This month holds good fortune for proceeding with something new or expanding
9th Month Oct 8th - Nov 7th	Be on guard. It is easy to get involved in conflict with others.
10th Month Nov 8th - Dec 6th	Luck and harmony are in sync. You will receive unexpected benefits by working with others.
11th Month Dec 7th - Jan 5th	A powerful sign of luck. Hard work will achieve favorable results.
12th Month Jan 6th - Feb 3rd	Luck is neither auspicious nor inauspicious.

The Ox

1925, 1937, 1949, 1961, 1973, 1985, 1997, 2009

Note: The New Year begins February 4th

2011 is not a time for the Ox to be speculative. Risky investments and business deals are not to be taken at face value. 2011 will seem unusually long to the Ox because of their moodiness. The Ox can expect to see some visible changes on the career front. While the nature of the transition is unpredictable, and unexpected problems may frequently arise, it is not a wise decision to look for a new venture or change in the Rabbit year. Finances could be your weakest area this year. That is not to say your prospects are gloomy, only that where money matters are concerned, you could be prone to large fluctuations. Your best strategy is to save as much as you can so you can afford some major expenses that are almost certain to present themselves. Do some soul-searching around your budget and determine the things that are important to you; try to minimize those expenses you deem less important. Don't be a guarantor or lend money to anyone so you can avoid having a relationship go sour. Your health will generally be good and there are no signs of major illness. To be safe, stay away from abusing alcohol or over-indulging in sex. The single Ox may experience mood swings and a fruitless search for romance this year. Quarrels will be easily aroused for married Oxen.

Your Benefactor is: Dog
(1922, 1934, 1946, 1958, 1970, 1982, 1994, 2006)

12 Month Outlook For The Ox

Solar Month	Comments
1st Month Feb 4th - Mar 5th	Watch out for documentation errors. This is not a good time to sign contracts.
2nd Month Mar 6th - Apr 4th	Be cautious of your health and do not visit sick people.
3rd Month Apr 5th - May 5th	Luck is steadily going up and good opportunities come your way.
4th Month May 6th - June 5th	Easy to get stabbed in the back. Make friends with caution.
5th Month June 6th - July 6th	Keep on high alert. Be less social. Avoid going out late to prevent being robbed.
6th Month July 7th - Aug 7th	This month holds good fortune for money prospects.
7th Month Aug 8th - Sept 7th	Luck is increasing. A benefactor may show up with unexpected good news.
8th Month Sept 8th - Oct 7th	Pay attention to your health to avoid minor illness.
9th Month Oct 8th - Nov 7th	Smooth sailing! Things are enjoyable with good results.
10th Month Nov 8th - Dec 6th	This is a great time to expand; start a new project.
11th Month Dec 7th - Jan 5th	Be humble. There are signs of conflict and fighting.
12th Month Jan 6th - Feb 3rd	Fortune is good. Proceed with any good idea or plan.

The Tiger

1926, 1938, 1950, 1962, 1974, 1986, 1998, 2010

Note: The New Year begins February 4th

This year lacks auspiciousness for the Tigers. There is no big leap this year. Things appear normal, but hidden dangers exist. It is definitely not the year to go fishing on a rough ocean. You have to examine the current situation carefully. Don't make any risky moves if you want to avoid losses. Don't make rushed decisions; think twice before acting. Focus on cooperative endeavors and cultivate friends and associates carefully. There are signs of disharmony in relationships with people. Money may come in abundantly, and leave abundantly. If you are careless, there will be a financial crisis. Don't gamble with your money or make any risky deals. While an inauspicious Guan Fu Star shines above, it is easy to encounter legal problems, lawsuits, or even imprisonment. Tolerance is the keyword. Try to take care of everything in person, and be humble at all times to prevent nasty situations. Because the Sickness Star is at your door, you and your family members may fall sick for no apparent reason. Stay away from the sick and don't visit the hospital if possible. Romance will be easy come, easy go. To avoid being cheated, refrain from giving too much in a relationship. There is the danger of married couples getting involved in scandalous affairs.

Your Benefactor is: Horse
(1930, 1942, 1954, 1966, 1978, 1990, 2002)

Solar Month	Comments
1st Month Feb 4th - Mar 5th	Average luck. Watch out for the flu or cuts.
2nd Month Mar 6th - Apr 4th	Powerful sign of luck. Hard work will achieve favorable results.
3rd Month Apr 5th - May 5th	Luck is neither auspicious nor inauspicious.
4th Month May 6th - June 5th	Beneficial to travel. You will have new opportunities.
5th Month June 6th - July 6th	This is a rewarding month for both romance and business.
6th Month July 7th - Aug 7th	Things are average to good. You may receive some unexpected benefit from your hard work.
7th Month Aug 8th - Sept 7th	This month can bring conflict and tension. Keep calm and say less.
8th Month Sept 8th - Oct 7th	Auspicious luck. The harder you work, the more you will gain.
9th Month Oct 8th - Nov 7th	A rewarding month. Most things are to your satisfaction.
10th Month Nov 8th - Dec 6th	Though there is pressure on your job, things will be relatively peaceful.
11th Month Dec 7th - Jan 5th	An especially good month for artists and writers! Also, this is the strongest Peach Blossom time.
12th Month Jan 6th - Feb 3rd	Luck and mood is like a bouncing ball – high and low.

It is not your position that
makes you happy or unhappy,
it is your disposition

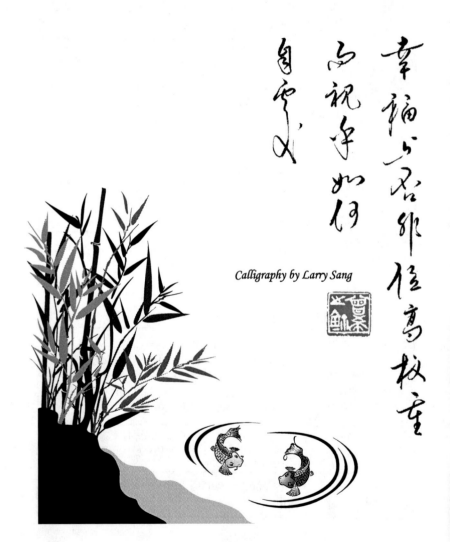

Calligraphy by Larry Sang

Li Ming

TABLE 1

LI MING (establish fate): STEP 1: DETERMINE YOUR PALACE

LI MING for 2011

立命

This is another system for making annual predictions:

☆ First, use Table 1, based on your month and time of birth.
☆ Take the results of Table 1, and use them in Table 2, along with your year of birth, to find the palace of Li Ming for 2011.
☆ Once you know the palace of Li Ming, read the prediction that follows for that palace.

Birth Hour:		Born After:											
		Jan 21 1st Month	Feb 19 2nd Month	Mar 20 3rd Month	Apr 20 4th Month	May 21 5th Month	Jun 21 6th Month	Jul 23 7th Month	Aug 23 8th Month	Sep 23 9th Month	Oct 23 10th Month	Nov 22 11th Month	Dec 22 12th Month
Zi	11pm-1am	Mao	Yin	Chou	Zi	Hai	Xu	You	Shen	Wei	Wu	Si	Chen
Chou	1-3am	Yin	Chou	Zi	Hai	Xu	You	Shen	Wei	Wu	Si	Chen	Mao
Yin	3-5am	Chou	Zi	Hai	Xu	You	Shen	Wei	Wu	Si	Chen	Mao	Yin
Mao	5-7am	Zi	Hai	Xu	You	Shen	Wei	Wu	Si	Chen	Mao	Yin	Chou
Chen	7-9am	Hai	Xu	You	Shen	Wei	Wu	Si	Chen	Mao	Yin	Chou	Zi
Si	9-11am	Xu	You	Shen	Wei	Wu	Si	Chen	Mao	Yin	Chou	Zi	Hai
Wu	11am-1pm	You	Shen	Wei	Wu	Si	Chen	Mao	Yin	Chou	Zi	Hai	Xu
Wei	1-3pm	Shen	Wei	Wu	Si	Chen	Mao	Yin	Chou	Zi	Hai	Xu	You
Shen	3-5pm	Wei	Wu	Si	Chen	Mao	Yin	Chou	Zi	Hai	Xu	You	Shen
You	5-7pm	Wu	Si	Chen	Mao	Yin	Chou	Zi	Hai	Xu	You	Shen	Wei
Xu	7-9pm	Si	Chen	Mao	Yin	Chou	Zi	Hai	Xu	You	Shen	Wei	Wu
Hai	9-11pm	Che	Mao	Yin	Chou	Zi	Hai	Xu	You	Shen	Wei	Wu	Si

Notes:

These months are different from the solar (Feng Shui/Four Pillars) months, and also are different from the lunar months. They begin on the *Qi* of the *Twenty-Four Jieqi*. If born within a day of these month dates, please consult a *Ten-Thousand Year Calendar* to determine exactly which is your birth month in this system. It is not necessary for you to understand the Chinese terms in the tables. Just follow the tables to the correct palace for you.

TABLE 2 立命 LI MING (establish fate): STEP 2: PALACE FOR A MAO (RABBIT) YEAR 立命 LI MING for 2011

Li Ming:	Birth Year:											
	Rat Zi	Ox Chou	Tiger Yin	Rabbit Mao	Dragon Chen	Snake Si	Horse Wu	Sheep Wei	Monkey Shen	Rooster You	Dog Xu	Pig Hai
Zi	You	Xu	Hai	Zi	Chou	Yin	Mao	Chen	Si	Wu	Wei	Shen
Chou	Xu	Hai	Zi	Chou	Yin	Mao	Chen	Si	Wu	Wei	Shen	You
Yin	Hai	Zi	Chou	Yin	Mao	Chen	Si	Wu	Wei	Shen	You	Xu
Mao	Zi	Chou	Yin	Mao	Chen	Si	Wu	Wei	Shen	You	Xu	Hai
Chen	Chou	Yin	Mao	Chen	Si	Wu	Wei	Shen	You	Xu	Hai	Zi
Si	Yin	Mao	Chen	Si	Wu	Wei	Shen	You	Xu	Hai	Zi	Chou
Wu	Mao	Chen	Si	Wu	Wei	Shen	You	Xu	Hai	Zi	Chou	Yin
Wei	Chen	Si	Wu	Wei	Shen	You	Xu	Hai	Zi	Chou	Yin	Mao
Shen	Si	Wu	Wei	Shen	You	Xu	Hai	Zi	Chou	Yin	Mao	Chen
You	Wu	Wei	Shen	You	Xu	Hai	Zi	Chou	Yin	Mao	Chen	Si
Xu	Wei	Shen	You	Xu	Hai	Zi	Chou	Yin	Mao	Chen	Si	Wu
Hai	Shen	You	Xu	Hai	Zi	Chou	Yin	Mao	Chen	Si	Wu	Wei

Notes:

☆ Take the Palace of Li Ming, found in Table 1, and compare it to the year of birth to find the palace for 2011, a Mao (Rabbit) year.

☆ Use January 21st as the beginning of the new year for finding the birth year. If the date falls within one day of January 21st, check in a *Ten-Thousand Year Calendar* to be sure. If the birth date is between January 1st and January 20th, consider the person as belonging to the previous year in this system.

☆ The predictions described below go from January 20th, 2011 until January 19th, 2012.

37

Li Ming Palace Reading

Zi

The year will begin with a fortunate trine aspect linking Wen Chang, Tian De and Fu Xing. Dreams can come true regarding financial or love matters. Be prudent and realistic, and then work hard to accomplish your goals. It is going to be a beautiful year for romance. Those who are married should avoid getting involved in extramarital affairs.

Chou

Li Ming here means a year to be conservative and not to be aggressive when embarking on a new career. Be forewarned of some obstacles you may encounter. There is lots of confusion in dealing with things. Money prospects alternate between good and bad. Investments should be made only after careful consideration. With Yue Sha star in this palace, avoid visiting the sick and attending funerals.

Yin

The inauspicious Wu Gui and Guan Fu stars make this an unstable year. If Li Ming is here, it is a time of floating and sinking. Where money is concerned, gains will not be proportional to the effort invested. Be practical in whatever you do. Conflict with others and tangled business dealings will arise easily. Be careful of legal affairs and be extra caution when signing contracts. Stay away from places where there are activities involving alcohol or gambling.

Mao

With Li Ming here, change is the theme of 2011. Be prepared to welcome these changes without clinging to what used to be. It is not a year to expand or to be overly optimistic. Money comes and goes easily. Be cautious of being betrayed by friends. There is a sign of bleeding. It will be easy to have some sort of injury by sharp metal objects. Teenagers should stay away from dangerous places to avoid injuries.

Chen

If Li Ming is here, you will find this year a blessed one. Good news can be expected within the family. Career and money prospects are in your favor. Salaried workers can look forward to a promotion or raise, and the self-employed can expand their business. Yet, be alert for signs over-spending or backstabbers. Do not trust anyone blindly lest you get cheated.

Si

If Li Ming is here, the whole year is safe and sound. Good money-making opportunities for the self-employed can be expected. This is a year to start any of your plans that can help you achieve long-term goals and lay a firm foundation for the future. However, there are signs of conflict in relationships. Restrain yourself and be prudent in all matters to avoid ruining your relationship. Avoiding gambling or financial speculation, as it will be a losing game.

Wu

With two auspicious stars shining above - Tian Xi and Yu Tang - you will find this year a blessed one. Good news can be expected within the family. Career and money prospects are promising. Luck is smooth for everything you plan. Most projects will hit the target. Seize this opportunity to take a big step forward and build your lifetime foundation. Watch out for robbery or backstabbers. It is not beneficial to stay out late at night.

Wei

Except for Hua Gai, a star of literature, there are no other auspicious stars. This is a good year for artists and writers. There are prospects for those working in creative fields and good academic results for those still in school. For others, this year indicates that work will require double the effort to receive a single gain. Be satisfied with small gains – don't expect too much. Think carefully before you invest in anything. Try not to set high financial expectations.

Shen Because a number of inauspicious stars gather, if Li Ming is here your fortune alternates between good and bad. Be practical in whatever you do. In business dealings, it will be easy to get tangled up. Pay more attention to your relationships with people. Tact and tolerance are needed to avoid friction with co-workers or someone close to you. Be on guard to prevent financial mishaps. There are signs of unnecessary expenditures.

You This year the Sui Po is in Ming along with other inauspicious stars, so it is appropriate to be cautious and prudent in all matters. This year is not a time to be speculative. Be careful of bleeding or injury by sharp metallic objects. Be alert for the big consumer Da Hao star. Do not trust anyone blindly lest you get cheated. However, the presence of Yi Ma and Lu Cun together bring good prospects for venturing overseas in your career.

Xu If Li Ming is here, two auspicious stars - Zi Wei and Long De - shine above, so all four seasons bring peace and prosperity. Both males and females can increase their blessings. This is a highly rewarding year. Career and money prospects are favorable. There are lots of opportunities waiting at the front door. Good fortune goes hand in hand with you, putting you in the right place at the right time. However, be cautious of a sudden financial mishap.

Hai If Li Ming is here, luck is unstable; it looks good, but there is bad hidden within. There are signs of conflict in career and lots of confusion in dealing with things. Sudden changes may throw your life into disarray. This is not a good time to expand or switch careers as you may end up worse off than before. With many temptations to spend, this year calls for careful financial management and restraint.

Liu Ren

Liu Ren (六壬)(小六壬)

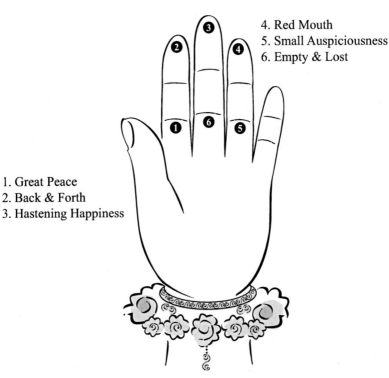

4. Red Mouth
5. Small Auspiciousness
6. Empty & Lost

1. Great Peace
2. Back & Forth
3. Hastening Happiness

CALCULATION:
When something out of the ordinary spontaneously happens,
you can determine the meaning of the omen with *Liu Ren*.
Here is the calculation:

1. Use the left hand. Start in position 1, Great Peace (大安 da an) and always move clockwise.
2. Count clockwise through the six positions for today's *lunar* month. The Great Peace position corresponds to the first lunar month. (Refer to the *Ten-Thousand Year Calendar* page at the end of this *Guide*. Find today's date, then read the month number at the top of the column.)
3. Count the position found in Step 2 as the first day of the lunar month. Count clockwise through the six positions to today, the current day of the lunar month. (Find today's date in the *Ten-Thousand Year Calendar* page, then read the day number on the side at the end of the row.)

4. Count the position found in Step 3 as the first double hour.
Count clockwise through the six positions to the current double hour.
5. Look up the interpretation of this palace on page 44-45.

HOUR TABLE		
Hour	During Standard Time	During Daylight Savings Time
1	11 pm - 1 am	midnight to 2 am
2	1 - 3 am	2 - 4 am
3	3 - 5 am	4 - 6 am
4	5 - 7 am	6 - 8 am
5	7 - 9 am	8 - 10 am
6	9 - 11 am	10 - noon
7	11 am - 1 pm	noon to 2 pm
8	1 - 3 pm	2 - 4 pm
9	3 - 5 pm	4 - 6 pm
10	5 - 7 pm	6 - 8 pm
11	7 - 9 pm	8 - 10 pm
12	9 - 11 pm	10 - midnight

Note: for 11 pm to midnight during standard time, use the next day's date.
For example, if it is 11:15 pm on February 12th, then count it as February 13th.

Example: April 8th, 2011, 10:15 am.
Start in Position One.
April 8th is in the column that says third month at the top.
So we go to Position Three.
April 8th is the sixth day of the third month.
Start where we left off in Position Three and call that 1.
Count clockwise to the 6th position from there: Position Two.
Start in Position Two and count for the hour.
Whether it is Daylight Savings Time or not, 10:15 am is the 6th hour.
Count 6 positions, with Position Two as the beginning, and end up in Position One.
This is the outcome:

Position One is Great Peace.
Read the text and apply it to the situation.

INTERPRETATION

1. Great Peace (大安 da an): The person in question has not moved at this time. This position belongs to wood element and the east. Generally in planning matters, use 1, 5, and 7. This position belongs to the four limbs. Helpful people are found in the southwest. Avoid the east. Children, women, and the six domestic animals are frightened.

In Great Peace, every activity prospers. Seek wealth in the southwest. Lost items are not far away. The house is secure and peaceful. The person you expect has not left yet. Illness is not serious. Military generals return home to the fields. Look for opportunities and push your luck.

2. Back and Forth (留連 liu lian): The person you expect is not returning yet. This position belongs to water element and the north. Generally in planning matters, use 2, 8, and 10. This position belongs to the kidneys and stomach. Helpful people are found in the south. Avoid the north. Children wander the road as disembodied spirits.

With Back and Forth, activities are difficult to achieve. You have not adequately planned for your goals. Official activities are delayed. Those who have gone do not return from their journey yet. Lost items appear in the south. Hurry and ask for what you want and you will get results. But guard against gossip and disputes. Family members for the moment are so-so.

3. Hastening Happiness (速喜 su xi):The expected person arrives shortly. This position belongs to fire element and the south. Generally in planning matters, use 3, 6, and 9. This position belongs to the heart and brain. Helpful people are found in the southwest. Avoid the south. Children, women, and animals are frightened.

With Hastening Happiness, happiness arrives. Seek wealth toward the south. Lost items are found between 11 a.m. and 5 p.m. if you ask a passerby about it. Official activities have blessing and virtue. Sick people have no misfortune. Auspicious for the fields, house, and the six livestock. You receive news from someone far away.

4. Red Mouth (赤口 chi kou): An inauspicious time for official activities. This position belongs to metal element and the west. Generally in planning matters, use 4, 7, and 10. This position belongs to the lungs and stomach. Helpful people are found in the east. Avoid the west. Children are bewildered young spirits.

Red Mouth governs quarrels and disputes. Be cautious about legal matters. Quickly go search for lost items. Travelers experience a fright. The six domestic animals give you trouble. The sick should go to the west. Furthermore, you must guard against being cursed. Fear catching epidemic diseases.

5. Small Auspiciousness (小吉 xiao ji): The expected person comes in a happy time. This position belongs to wood element and all directions. Generally in planning matters, use 1, 5, and 7. This position belongs to the liver and intestines. Helpful people are found in the southwest. Avoid the east. Children, women, and the six domestic animals are frightened.

Small Auspiciousness is most auspicious and prosperous. Your road is smooth. Spirits come announcing good news. Lost items are located in the southwest. Travelers promptly arrive. Relations with others are extremely strong. Everything is harmonious. A sick person should pray to heaven.

6. Empty and Lost (空亡 kong wang): News you expect does not come at this time. This position belongs to earth element. Generally in planning matters, use 3, 6, and 9. This position belongs to the spleen and brain. Helpful people are found in the north. Watch out for the health of your children. Males feel pressure. The activities of females get no results.

Spirits are often unreasonable or perverse. Seeking wealth is without benefit. There is disaster for travelers. Lost items will not appear. Official activities bring punishment and damage. Sick people meet a dark ghost. To be secure and peaceful, get release from calamity by sacrifice and prayer.

Example: You arrive at the airport, but your friend who was supposed to pick you up is not there and does not answer his cell phone. You use Liu Ren to find out what is going on.

Today's time and date: March 14th, 2011, 8:30 am

A. Start in Position One.

B. March 14th is in the column that says second month at the top. So we go to Position Two.
   March 14h is the tenth day of the second month.
   Start where we left off in Position Two and call that 1.

C. Count clockwise to the 10th position from there: Position Five.
   Start in Position Five and count for the hour.
   It is 8:30 a.m., the 5th hour.

D. Count 5 positions, with Position Five as the beginning, and end up in Position Three.

This is the outcome:

> **Position Three is Hastening Happiness**
> Read the text and apply it to the situation. Hastening Happiness begins with "The expected person arrives shortly." You wait calmly for ten minutes and your ride arrives. He tells you traffic delayed him and he forgot his cell phone.

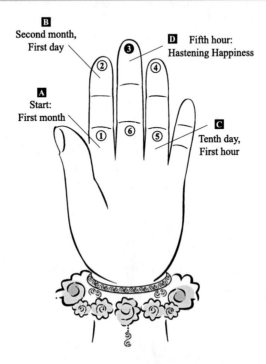

B
Second month, First day

D Fifth hour: Hastening Happiness

A Start: First month

C Tenth day, First hour

Omen

Omens

In Chinese almanacs, there are often listings of predictions based on omens. We include a few below. Have fun with it and don't take it too seriously.

Omens from the Twitch of an Eye		
Time	**Eye**	**This is an omen of:**
11pm-1am	left	Meeting a benefactor.
zi	right	Having a good meal.
1-3am	left	Having anxiety.
chou	right	Someone thinking about you.
3-5am	left	Someone coming from afar.
yin	right	A happy matter arriving.
5-7am	left	The coming of an important guest.
mao	right	Something peaceful, safe, and auspicious.
7-9am	left	A guest coming from afar.
chen	right	Injury or harm.
9-11am	left	Having a good meal.
si	right	Something inauspicious.
11am-1pm	left	Having a good meal.
wu	right	An inauspicious matter.
1-3pm	left	A lucky star.
wei	right	Good luck, but small.
3-5pm	left	Money coming.
shen	right	Someone thinking of you romantically.
5-7pm	left	A guest coming.
you	right	A guest arriving.
7-9pm	left	A guest arriving.
xu	right	A gathering or meeting.
9-11pm	left	A guest arriving.
hai	right	Gossip.

Correct for *Daylight Savings Time*, if in use (subtract one hour from the current time).

Omens from Hiccoughs	
Time	**This is an omen of:**
11pm-1am zi	A good meal and a happy dinner gathering.
1-3am chou	Someone missing you; a guest coming to seek your help.
3-5am yin	Someone missing you; a dining engagement.
5-7am mao	Wealth and happiness; someone coming to ask about a matter.
7-9am chen	A good meal; great good luck for everyone.
9-11am si	A lucky person coming to seek wealth.
11am-1pm wu	An important guest; someone wanting a dinner gathering.
1-3pm wei	Someone wanting a meal; lucky activities.
3-5pm shen	Nightmares; eating is not beneficial.
5-7pm you	Someone coming; someone asks about a matter.
7-9pm xu	Someone missing you; a meeting brings benefit.
9-11pm hai	Something frightens, but on the contrary, brings benefit.

Correct for *Daylight Savings Time*, if in use (subtract one hour from the current time).

最貧窮的不是身無分文，而是沒有夢想

Calligraphy by Larry Sang

The poorest one is not one without a cent but one without a DREAM

The Yellow Emperor

The Yellow Emperor in the Four Seasons

黃帝四季詩

Spring

Autumn

Summer

Winter

There is a lifetime prediction commonly found in Chinese almanacs. Based on your season of birth, find your birth time.

The Yellow Emperor in the Four Seasons

Time of Birth		Season of Birth			
		Spring February 4th to May 4th	**Summer** May 5th to August 6th	**Autumn** August 7th to November 6th	**Winter** November 7th to February 3rd
Zi	11p-1a	head	low abdomen	shoulders	low abdomen
Chou	1-3a	chest	hands	hands	knees
Yin	3-5a	feet	feet	knees	chest
Mao	5-7a	shoulders	shoulders	chest	shoulders
Chen	7-9a	knees	knees	feet	feet
Si	9-11a	hands	hands	hands	head
Wu	11a-1p	low abdomen	head	shoulders	hands
Wei	1-3p	hands	chest	chest	knees
Shen	3-5p	feet	feet	low abdomen	chest
You	5-7p	shoulders	shoulders	knees	shoulders
Xu	7-9p	knees	knees	feet	feet
Hai	9-11p	chest	chest	head	hands

Correct birth time for Daylight Saving Time, if used at the time of birth. If you were born in the Southern Hemisphere, switch the autumn and spring dates, as well as the summer and winter dates.

The Yellow Emperor in the Four Seasons

Born on the Yellow Emperor's head means a lifetime of never having worries. Even petty people have riches and honor. Clothes and food naturally come around. Your position in society is elevated, and gentlemen are good at planning. Women go through life steadily and smoothly, marrying a talented and educated person.

Born on the Yellow Emperor's hands means business capital is sufficient. Going out, you meet a benefactor. Inside the home, you have everything. Your early years are very steady and smooth. You accumulate many possesions. Wealth comes from every direction. When old, it is in your hands.

Born on the Yellow Emperor's shoulders means a life of a million riches. You have wealth in your middle years. Children and grandchildren are plenty. Clothes and income at all times are good. In old age, you have fields in the village. Siblings are helpful. Your early life is bitter, but the later end is sweet.

Born on the Yellow Emperor's chest means clothes and food are naturally ample. Experts in the pen and the sword are around you. There is music, song, and dance. Middle age brings good clothes and food. Later years are happy and prosperous. Joy, utmost honor, prosperity, and increased longevity add more blessings.

Born on the Yellow Emperor's lower abdomen, you were treasured by your parents. In middle age, clothes and food are good. When old you obtain gold. The family reputation is changing a lot. You are a noble person. Children and grandchildren must newly shine. Cultured and bright, they advance a lot.

Born on the Yellow Emperor's knees means doing things is without benefit. In your early years, you toiled a lot, but did not lack clothes and food. Every day, you travel on the road; you cannot avoid running back and forth. Old age is smooth, with honor and prosperity, but in middle age, hard work is extreme.

Born on the Yellow Emperor's feet, practice moral teachings to avoid toil. A lifetime that is safe and sound, but unsuitable to reside in your ancestor's home. Women marry two husbands. Men have two wives. Search lonely mountain ranges. Leave your homeland to achieve good fortune.

Feng Shui

Feng Shui

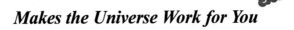

Makes the Universe Work for You

We live in a universe that is filled with different energies. Our planet rotates on its axis, creating cycles of day and night. The earth also revolves around the sun in yearly cycles and is subject to various gravitational and magnetic fields. Our solar system is moving through space and is also subject to other forces in the universe. These physical forces and many different time cycles affect us profoundly. The Chinese have spent centuries observing the effects of these forces, and learning how to better harmonize humans with their environment. This is the science and art of Feng Shui (Chinese geomancy).

Feng Shui uses observation, repeatable calculations and methodologies, and is based on the study of the environment, both inside and out of the house. Feng Shui can help you determine the best home to live in, which colors can enhance your home, the best bed positions for deep sleep, and how to change your business or home into a center of power. Feng Shui can help improve your health, your relationships and your prosperity. It is based on a complex calculation and observation of the environment, rather than a metaphysical reading relying on inspiration or intuition.

The American Feng Shui Institute publishes the annual Chinese Astrology and Feng Shui Guide so that both the Feng Shui professional and layperson can benefit from the knowledge of the incoming energy cycles and their influences. With this knowledge, one can adjust their environment to make it as harmonious as possible for the current year.

The following sections contain the energy patterns for the current year with an analysis and remedy for each of the eight directions. For the nonprofessional, there is a section on how to prepare your home for this reading. Please note that Feng Shui is a deep and complex science that requires many years to master. Preparing your home to receive the annual energy is one aspect that anyone can apply. A professional reading is recommended to anyone who wishes to receive the greatest benefits possible that Feng Shui can bring.

Preparing your home for a Feng Shui reading

The Floor Plan

The first requirement for preparing your home for a Feng Shui annual reading is to create a proportional floor plan. This plan can be hand drawn or be the original building plans, as long as the plan is proportionally correct. It is not necessary to draw in all your furniture except perhaps noting your bed and desk. It is important that you indicate where all window and door openings are.

**Example A
Floor plan**

**Example B
Floor plan**

Preparing your home for a Feng Shui reading

Gridding The Floor Plan

Once you have your floor plan drawn, you then overlay a 9- square grid. This grid is proportional to the floor plan. If it were a long and narrow house, so would the grid be long and narrow. You want to divide the floor plan into equal thirds both top to bottom and left to right as shown below:

**Example A
with grid**

**Example B
with grid**

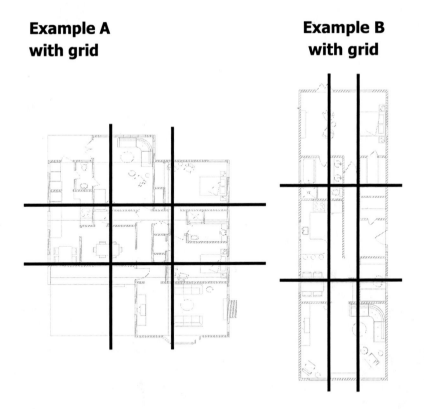

The Compass Reading

The next step is to determine the alignment of your house with the earth magnetic fields by taking a compass reading. It is very important to take an accurate reading and not guess the orientation based on the direction of the sun or a map.

Why Do You Need To Use A Compass?

In Feng Shui, we look at the eight cardinal and inter-cardinal directions: East, Southeast, South, Southwest, West, Northwest, North, and Northeast when analyzing a home or building. Each of these directions holds unique significance to these buildings. If you do not use a compass to determine the correct orientation, you might completely misread your home. You cannot map the qi within the building without an exact orientation. It is similar to finding your way out of a forest without a compass. You have a high probability of getting lost. Without a compass, it simply is not Feng Shui.

A Compass vs. A Luopan

You can use any compass if you do not have a Luopan. The Luopan is simply a Chinese compass that helps determine the sitting direction of a building. It also contains a wealth of information on its dial that is used for more advanced applications. In recent years, Master Larry Sang simplified the traditional Luopan specifically for training Western students. Although it looks simple compared to an original Luopan, it has all the tools you need to accurately analyze a building. An important fact to remember about a Luopan is that it points to the South. The following information and instructions apply to a Luopan, however, if you are using a Western compass these concepts are easy to adapt.

Sang's Luopan

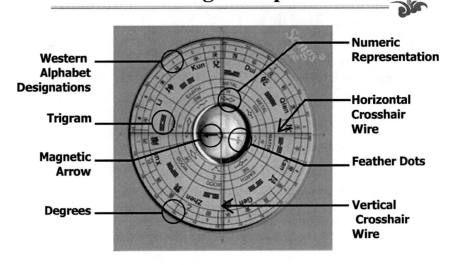

Western Alphabet Designations

Trigram

Magnetic Arrow

Degrees

Numeric Representation

Horizontal Crosshair Wire

Feather Dots

Vertical Crosshair Wire

Parts of Sang's Luopan

The Magnetic Arrow - The arrowhead points South rather than North. Western compasses point North.

The Feather Dots - (The twin dots at the center of the rotating dial). Always adjust the rotating (gold) dial to align the twin dots with the feather end of the arrow.

The Numeric Representations - The innermost ring has a dot pattern that represents the Trigrams' numbers. For example, Kun has two dots and Qian has six dots.

Crosshair Alignments - The red crosshairs designate the facing and sitting directions. Once the arrow is steady and the feather end is aligned over the north twin dots, you can determine the sitting direction and the facing direction.

The Eight Trigrams - The Eight Trigrams are the basis for orientation in Feng Shui and are shown on the Luopan with their respective elements, symbols, and directions.

Western Alphabet Designations - Each Trigram is divided into three equal parts. These parts are shown with both their Chinese symbols and using the Western Alphabet.

The Degrees - Outermost on the dial are the Western compass degrees in Arabic numerals.

General Guidelines for using the Luopan:

To use the Luopan or compass correctly, remember the following guidelines:

1. Always stand straight and upright.

2. Do not wear metal jewelry or belt buckles that can skew the compass.

3. Avoid any electrical influences such as automobiles or electrical boxes.

4. Always stand parallel to the building.

5. Keep your feet square below you.

6. You can keep the Luopan in the lower box case to manage it better.

Taking a reading with the Luopan:

With the general guidelines for using a luopan in mind, now you are ready to take a reading to determine which wall or corner of your home is located closest to North.

1. Take your reading outside, standing parallel to your home with your back to it. Stand straight and hold the Luopan at waist level. Wait until the arrow ceases to quiver.

2. Slowly turn the center (gold) dial so that the North/feather dots align with the feather of the arrow. If using a Western compass, turn the compass so that the needle's arrow end aligns with north (between 337.5 - 22.5 degrees).

3. Please take at least three separate readings from other positions. If you find that there is a discrepancy, take various readings at various locations until you are sure which one is correct. One direction should stand out as being correct.

4. Indicate on your floor plan which section is North. Fill in the other directions as illustrated. Please note that North can lie in a corner section.

Example A   **Example B**

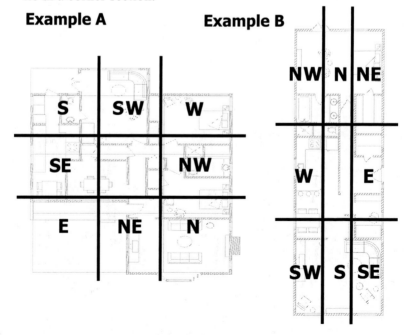

Directions to Avoid for Construction

The Three Sha and the Sui Po

The **Three Sha** are in the **West (Northwest and Southwest):**
Shen, You and **Xu** directions.

The **Sui Po** or **Year Breaker** is in the **West: You** direction.

The **Tai Sui** is in the **East: Mao** direction.

> Therefore, avoid using these directions:
> **Mao, Shen, You, and Xu**

Directions to Avoid

15° Direction	Degrees	45° Direction	Sang's Luopan Alpha Designation
Shen		SW	q
Geng			r
You	232.5° - 307.5°	W	s
Xin			t
Xu		NW	u
Mao	82.5° - 97.5°	E	g

What should we avoid in these directions?

- New construction sitting in these directions (except Mao East).
- Major renovation to buildings sitting in these directions (except Mao East).
- Major renovation to this section of the house, regardless of the sitting direction.
- Burial of the deceased in these directions.
- Digging or breaking of earth in these directions. If digging cannot be avoided in any of these areas, then place a metal wind chime outside between the house and the digging site.
- In addition, Rabbits or Roosters born in the second, fifth, or eighth month of the Chinese calendar should avoid attending funerals or burials.

Feng Shui
2011

Qi Pattern

SE ䷭ 6 White	**S** ䷟ 2 Black	**SW** ䷆ 4 Green
E ䷗ 5 Yellow	7 Red	**W** ䷂ 9 Purple
NE ䷓ 1 White	**N** ䷏ 3 Jade	**NW** ䷬ 8 White

The Qi (energy) shift begins on

February 4th, 2011 at 12:32 pm

Introduction

While this diagram may look foreign to the beginner, it is essential information for the experienced Feng Shui practitioner. Each year the qi pattern brings different effects. Some of these effects are quite auspicious and favorable and some may be inauspicious and not so favorable.

The effects of the 2011 energy pattern are analyzed for you in the following pages. Each analysis contains suggested remedies or enhancements for each section. Remedies are recommended to reduce negative qi. Enhancements are recommended to increase beneficial qi. These remedies or enhancements consist of the five elements: wood, fire, earth, metal, and water.

To use a remedy or enhancement, it must be placed inside the house within that particular section. If more than one room exists within a section, then each room needs to have its own remedy or enhancement. Any exceptions will be noted.

Feng Shui

2011

SE ䷗ 6 White	**S** ䷜ 2 Black	**SW** ䷁ 4 Green
E ䷗ 5 Yellow	**Fighting** *Po Jun* 7 Red	**W** ䷗ 9 Purple
NE ䷗ 1 White	**N** ䷗ 3 Jade	**NW** ䷗ 8 White

The Center Section

Center

Analysis

Last year (2010), we saw that the **8 White Zuo Fu Star** visited the center. We predicted that Mountain above Mountain forms hexagram 52, *Gen Gua*. The meaning of this hexagram is "Keeping still; impediment." The world was entering an era of "slower growth" and economic recovery would be slow and painful.

In 2011, the **7 Red Po Jun Star** visits the center. We are currently in Period 8, so the 8 White (earth element) star is in the center, and is productive to 7 Red Po Jun (metal). From this, we can predict that this year the world enters another era of "growth of fighting and conflict." Economic recovery may still be slow and painful. The weakness in the labor market will persist for longer than we would like. But adjusting to the new economic realities will smooth the transition from recession to recovery.

Together **8 white** and **7 red** form **Sun,** Hexagram 41 in the *Yi Jing*. The meaning of this hexagram is "to decrease" or "to reduce." Decrease does not always mean something bad. Increase and decrease come in their own time. What matters here is to understand the time and not to try to cover up poverty with empty pretense.

Feng Shui

2011

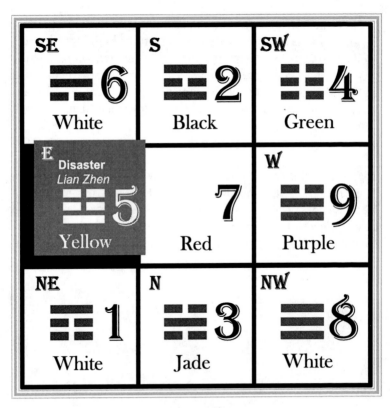

SE	S	SW
☴ **6** White	☷ **2** Black	☶ **4** Green
E Disaster *Lian Zhen* ☵ **5** Yellow	**7** Red	W ☱ **9** Purple
NE ☶ **1** White	N ☳ **3** Jade	NW ☰ **8** White

The East Section

East

Situation

Doors, bedrooms, or study rooms in the east section.

Analysis

This year the *5 Yellow Lian Zhen Disaster Star* falls into the east. This is a sign of potential for delays, obstacles, fire, lawsuits, sickness, and casualties. The 5 yellow star is earth element. The east section is the home of the *3 Jade Lu Cun Star*. The *3 Jade Lu Cun Star* is related to gossip, lawsuits and robbery. The *Lu Cun Star* is wood element. Wood dominates Earth, so the East section is definitely not an auspicious area. Moreover, the Sui Sha is in the east also, so if unfortunately the main entrance or bedroom is located in this section and no remedy is applied, an unexpected casualty is quite possible. It is advisable to avoid spending a lot of time in this area. In the east section, ground digging should especially be avoided to prevent the occurrence of misfortune.

Remedy

To reduce the potential negative effects, use metal element as a remedy in this section. A metal remedy can consist of metal décor such as a piece of sculpture. An ornament that has moving metal parts is preferable, such as a grandfather clock.

Caution

Do not allow construction or ground digging.

Feng Shui 2011

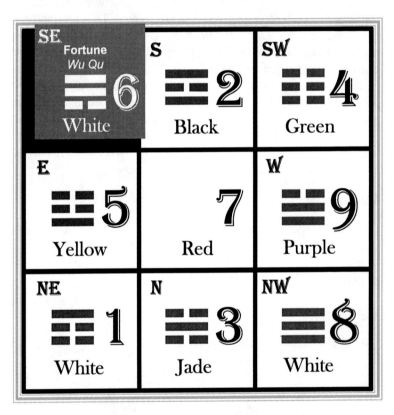

SE Fortune *Wu Qu* **6** White	**S** **2** Black	**SW** **4** Green
E **5** Yellow	**7** Red	**W** **9** Purple
NE **1** White	**N** **3** Jade	**NW** **8** White

The Southeast Section

Southeast

Situation

Doors, bedrooms, study rooms in the southeast section.

Analysis

The *6 Fortune Star* visits the southeast in 2011. The *6 Fortune Star* is sharp yang metal. The southeast section is the home of the *4 Green Wen Qu Literary Star*, which is wood element. The combination of the wood of 4 Green and the metal of 6 White creates a domination relationship. This makes the southeast section not beneficial for artists, writers and people working in entertainment business. There is also the potential of injuries to the thighs or pain at the waist. A female whose bedroom is in this section easily receives some kind of cheating heart romance. However, you can make use of the water element to change the above mentioned negative qi into positive qi.

Caution

Not beneficial for artists, writers and people working in the entertainment business. Easy to receive unhappy romance.

Remedy

Use water element as a remedy in this section. A fountain or aquarium in the southeast will help to change the poison into medicine.

After Remedy

It will bring strong romance qi (peach blossom) and good results in academia, for students, writers, and people working in the entertainment industry.

Feng Shui 2011

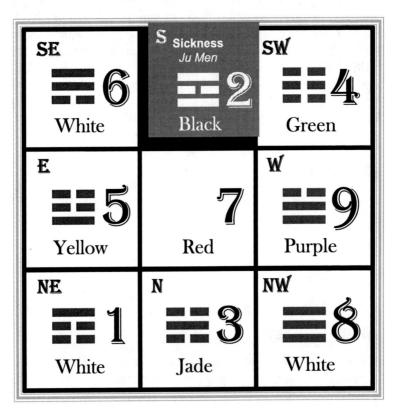

SE **6** White	**S** Sickness *Ju Men* **2** Black	SW **4** Green
E **5** Yellow	**7** Red	W **9** Purple
NE **1** White	N **3** Jade	NW **8** White

The South Section

South

Situation

Doors, bedrooms, study rooms in the south section.

Analysis

The *2 Black Ju Men Star* visits the south this year. 2 Black is earth element. The south is associated with fire. Fire feeds 2 Black earth, making the illness qi strong. Therefore, this area is not good for your main entrance, bedroom or for lots of activity. If a female's bedroom is in the south, it is particularly easy to be stricken by illness. Pregnant women should take every precaution against miscarriage by avoiding spending time or using a door in the south.

Remedy

Use metal element in your décor to reduce the unhealthy *2 Black Sickness* energy.

Caution

Pregnant women should avoid using the south section.

Feng Shui

2011

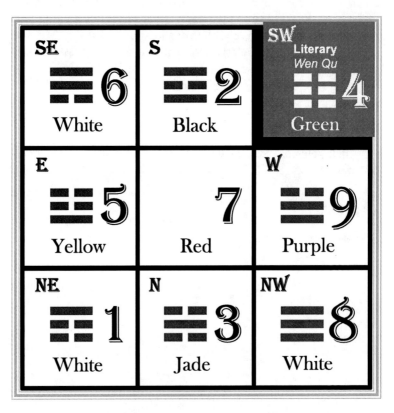

SE ䷗ **6** White	**S** ䷁ **2** Black	**SW** *Literary* *Wen Qu* **4** Green
E **5** Yellow	**7** Red	**W** **9** Purple
NE **1** White	**N** **3** Jade	**NW** **8** White

The Southwest Section

Southwest

Situation

Doors, bedrooms, study rooms in the southwest section.

Analysis

This year the *4 Green Literary Star* visits the southwest. 4 Green is related to wood. The southwest is earth element. Wood dominates earth. The auspicious stars San He and Hua Gai together make southwest strong for Peach Blossoms (romance and social relationships), especially for males to attract a female. Also, good for artists and people in entertainment industry. However, under influence of the inauspicious star *Jie Sha* (Robbery) Star, be on guard for unexpected casualties or break-ins. Avoid ground digging.

Remedy

Put water in a metal container in the southwest to cancel the domination relationship and enhance the 4 green literary Wen Qu Star.

Benefits

Beneficial for writers, artists, public relationships, or entertainment-related businesses, such as bars, nightclubs and casinos. Strong for Peach Blossom.

Caution

Be wary of excessive Peach Blossom that may lead to problems for married couples.

Feng Shui

2011

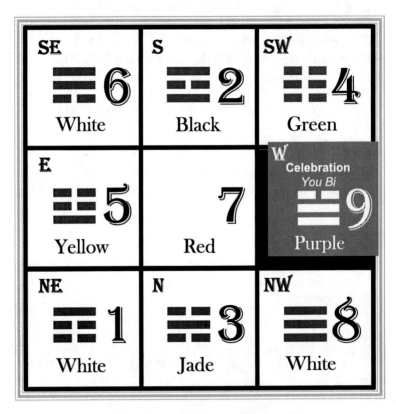

SE	S	SW
6 White	2 Black	4 Green
E 5 Yellow	7 Red	W Celebration *You Bi* 9 Purple
NE 1 White	N 3 Jade	NW 8 White

The West Section

West

Situation

Doors, bedrooms, study rooms in the west section.

Analysis

The *9 Purple Celebration Star* is in the west this year. This Celebration Star gathers together with yearly auspicious stars such as the Long De and Zi Wei, making this section strong in peach blossom and money luck. Make use of this section, it will be quite beneficial for the self-employed to expand their business while salaried workers easily gain promotions. Yet, the *Sui Sha* and *Da Hao* inauspicious stars are also in the west; therefore, if the main entrance falls in this section you should be careful of conflict with others or money loss and be on guard against unexpected casualty because of sex.

Benefits

Beneficial for expanding business, gaining recognition and getting new family members. Strong peach blossom.

Caution

Due to **Three Sha** in the west, avoid ground digging or construction.

Feng Shui
2011

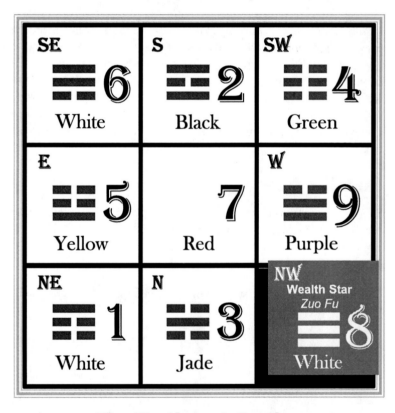

SE	S	SW
6 White	**2** Black	**4** Green
E **5** Yellow	**7** Red	**W** **9** Purple
NE **1** White	**N** **3** Jade	**NW** Wealth Star *Zuo Fu* **8** White

The Northwest Section

Northwest

Situation

Doors, bedrooms, study rooms in the northwest section.

Analysis

The *8 White Zuo Fu Money Star* is in the northwest section this year. It brings fame and wealth. The 8 White Zuo Fu Money Star is earth. The northwest is the home of the *6 White Fortune Star*, which is metal element. The productive relationship of earth and metal make this section quite excellent. In Feng Shui, *6 White and 8 White* together means "when Heaven comes to Mountain, become a billionaire." These two White Fortune stars together make the northwest a wealth-making and power-enhancing section. However, due to an inauspicious star, *Disaster Sha*, avoid ground digging to prevent conflicts and the occurrence of misfortune

Benefits

Beneficial for politicians to extend power and businessmen to expand their business.

Caution

Avoid ground digging to prevent conflicts; arguments and misunderstandings are easily aroused between young and old people.

Feng Shui

2011

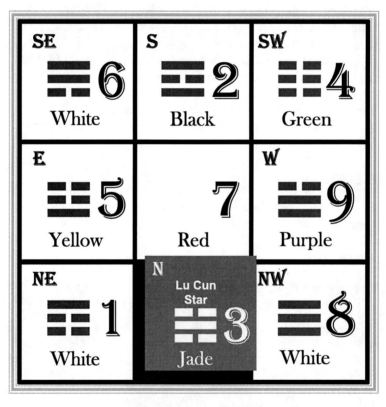

SE	S	SW
6 White	**2** Black	**4** Green
E		W
5 Yellow	**7** Red	**9** Purple
NE	N Lu Cun Star	NW
1 White	**3** Jade	**8** White

The North Section

North

Situation

Doors, bedrooms, study rooms in the north section.

Analysis

The 3 *Jade Lu Cun Star* falls into the north. This 3 Jade star is wood element, it is associated with aggression, expansion, gossip and legal problems. The north is the home of the **1 White Fortune Star**, and it is water element. The 1 White (water) and the 3 Jade (wood) are in a production relationship. 1 White and 3 Jade plus auspicious stars like Fu Xing and Tian De in the north make this section very strong for self-motivation and moving forward. However, a number of inauspicious stars, such as Gossip and Tangle Sha, gather in the north; therefore it is not advisable to have running water in this section to prevent the occurrence of misfortunes such as lawsuits, break-ins or robbery.

Benefits

Beneficial for attorneys, law firms, brokers, and sales.

Caution

No running water in the north.

Feng Shui

2011

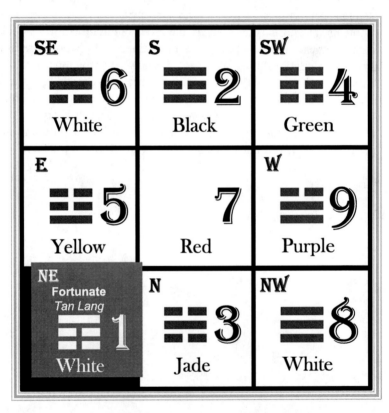

SE	S	SW
6 White	2 Black	4 Green
E 5 Yellow	7 Red	W 9 Purple
NE Fortunate *Tan Lang* 1 White	N 3 Jade	NW 8 White

The Northeast Section

Northeast

Situation

Doors, bedrooms, study rooms in the northeast section.

Analysis

The *1 White Fortune Star* visits the northeast section this year. 1 White is water element. This star represents wealth and Peach Blossom. The northeast is the home of the *8 White Zuo Fu Money Star* which also brings fame and wealth. Its element is earth. 1 white and 8 white have a domination relationship. Even though these two fortune and money star are hand in hand, there are inauspicious stars like Guan Fu and Bing Fu in this section. Because of this, it is not advisable to do any kind of risky investment or work too much. No doubt, this section will produce a lot of wealth opportunities, but it is easy to arouse legal problems, sex scandals and to be stricken by illness too.

Caution

Not beneficial for over-aggressive expansion. Stay away from extramarital affairs and avoid visiting sick people.

Remedy

Always keep this area clean and bright. Put in metal element to change the domination relationship into a productive relationship.

When you lose,
don't lose the lesson

Calligraphy by
Larry Sang

Day Selection

Day Selection

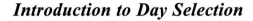

Introduction to Day Selection

Day Selection has been used for a long time in China. Every year, almanacs would be published giving the best days for important activities, as well as days to avoid. It is thought that a positive outcome is more likely when an activity is begun on an auspicious day. In English, we talk about getting things off to a good start, but have no particular methodology to do this.

There are three aspects to selecting a good day: picking a day that is good for the activity, avoiding a day that is bad for the activity, and picking a day that is not bad for the person(s) involved. In the calendar pages that follow, each day will list two or three activities that are auspicious or inauspicious on that day. If you wanted to pick a date to get married, you would first look for days that were considered good for weddings. In addition, you need to check the birth information of the bride and groom. If the bride is a Rabbit and the groom is a Rat, then you also need to avoid any days that say Bad for Rat or Bad for Rabbit, even if they are good for weddings in general.

In addition, there are some days that are not good for any important activity. Usually this is because the energy of heaven and earth is too strong or inharmonious on those days.

Day Selection is used for the first day of an activity. It does not affect a continued activity. For example, you should begin construction on a day that is good for groundbreaking, but it is not a problem if the construction is continued through a day that is bad for groundbreaking. The construction need not be stopped.

On the next page are definitions of the various activities included in Master Sang's Day Selection Calendar.

Calender Terminology Key

Animals:
Generally a bad day for a person born in the year of the animal listed. Even if an activity is listed as beneficial for that day, it will usually not be beneficial for that animal.

Begin Mission:
Beginning a new position, mission, or assignment.

Burial:
Burial.

Business:
Trade or business.

Buy Property:
Purchasing real estate.

Contracts:
Signing or entering into a contract, pact, or agreement.

Don't Do Important things:
A bad day for most activities.

Fix House:
Repairing the inside or outside of the house. Also for installing major appliances, such as the stove or oven.

Grand Opening:
Good or bad for opening a new business, restaurant, etc. Opening ceremonies for a new event.

Funeral:
Funerals.

Ground Breaking:
Beginning construction or disturbing the earth.

Healing:
Curing diseases, beginning a course of treatment.

Lawsuits:
Filing a lawsuit or going to court.

Moving:
Moving or changing residences.

Planting:
Gardening or planting.

Prayer:
Praying for blessings or happiness.

School:
Admissions into a new school.

Travel:
Going out or beginning a trip.

Wedding:
Marriage ceremonies or becoming engaged to be married.

Worship:
Rituals, rites, ceremonies, offering sacrifices, or honoring ancestors or the dead.

S	M	T	W	T	F	S
						1
2	3	4	5	6	7	8
9	10	11	12	13	14	15
16	17	18	19	20	21	22
23	24	25	26	27	28	29
30	31					

January 2011

Unfavorable for:

Sat **1**	**Good for:** Business, begin mission, wedding *Bad for: Lawsuit, travel*	*Dog*
Sun **2**	**Good for:** Prayer, worship *Bad for: Grand opening, ground breaking*	*Pig*
Mon **3**	⊖ **DON'T DO IMPORTANT THINGS** ⊖	*Rat*
Tue **4**	**Good for:** Planting, prayer *Bad for: Begin mission, grand opening, wedding*	*Ox*
Wed **5**	⊖ **DON'T DO IMPORTANT THINGS** ⊖	*Tiger*
Thu **6**	**Good for:** Business, grand opening, wedding *Bad for: Lawsuit, moving*	*Rabbit*
Fri **7**	**Good for:** Prayer, worship *Bad for: Grand opening, burial*	*Dragon*
Sat **8**	**Good for:** Planting, prayer *Bad for: Begin mission, wedding*	*Snake*
Sun **9**	**Good for:** Burial, ground breaking *Bad for: Lawsuit, grand opening*	*Horse*
Mon **10**	**Good for:** Worship, contracts *Bad for: Ground breaking*	*Sheep*
Tue **11**	**Good for:** Planting, school *Bad for: Grand opening, wedding*	*Monkey*
Wed **12**	**Good for:** Prayer, worship *Bad for: Begin mission, grand opening*	*Rooster*
Thu **13**	**Good for:** Worship *Bad for: Ground breaking, wedding*	*Dog*
Fri **14**	**Good for:** Fix house, business, contracts *Bad for: Burial, ground breaking*	*Pig*
Sat **15**	**Good for:** Begin mission, moving, wedding *Bad for: Lawsuit, funeral*	*Rat*

Sun **16**	⊜ **DON'T DO IMPORTANT THINGS** ⊜	*Ox*
Mon **17**	⊜ **DON'T DO IMPORTANT THINGS** ⊜	*Tiger*
Tue **18**	**Good for:** Grand opening, school, wedding *Bad for: Fix house, burial*	*Rabbit*
Wed **19**	**Good for:** Prayer, worship *Bad for: Grand opening, wedding*	*Dragon*
Thu **20**	**Good for:** Ground breaking, worship *Bad for: Lawsuit, fix house*	*Snake*
Fri **21**	**Good for:** Burial, worship *Bad for: Moving, grand opening*	*Horse*
Sat **22**	⊜ **DON'T DO IMPORTANT THINGS** ⊜	*Sheep*
Sun **23**	**Good for:** Fix house, travel *Bad for: Begin mission, grand opening*	*Monkey*
Mon **24**	**Good for:** Planting, prayer *Bad for: Lawsuit, moving*	*Rooster*
Tue **25**	**Good for:** Prayer, worship *Bad for: Begin mission, grand opening*	*Dog*
Wed **26**	**Good for:** Begin mission, business, contracts *Bad for: Ground breaking, lawsuit*	*Pig*
Thu **27**	**Good for:** Contracts, wedding *Bad for: Moving, burial*	*Rat*
Fri **28**	⊜ **DON'T DO IMPORTANT THINGS** ⊜	*Ox*
Sat **29**	⊜ **DON'T DO IMPORTANT THINGS** ⊜	*Tiger*
Sun **30**	**Good for:** Grand opening, wedding, buy property *Bad for: Lawsuit*	*Rabbit*
Mon **31**	**Good for:** Prayer, worship *Bad for: Begin mission, grand opening, wedding*	*Dragon*

S	M	T	W	T	F	S
		1	2	3	4	5
6	7	8	9	10	11	12
13	14	15	16	17	18	19
20	21	22	23	24	25	26
27	28					

February 2011

Unfavorable for:

Tue **1**	⊖ **DON'T DO IMPORTANT THINGS** ⊖	*Snake*
Wed **2**	**Good for:** prayer, worship *Bad for: grand opening, wedding, fix house*	*Horse*
Thu **3**	⊖ **DON'T DO IMPORTANT THINGS** ⊖	*Sheep*
Fri **4**	**Good for:** prayer, contracts *Bad for: burial*	*Monkey*
Sat **5**	**Good for:** grand opening, wedding, begin mission	*Rooster*
Sun **6**	**Good for:** burial, grand opening, ground breaking	*Dog*
Mon **7**	⊖ **DON'T DO IMPORTANT THINGS** ⊖	*Pig*
Tue **8**	**Good for:** grand opening, moving, wedding	*Rat*
Wed **9**	**Good for:** prayer, worship	*Ox*
Thu **10**	**Good for:** prayer	*Tiger*
Fri **11**	⊖ **DON'T DO IMPORTANT THINGS** ⊖	*Rabbit*
Sat **12**	**Good for:** prayer, worship *Bad for: wedding, grand opening*	*Dragon*
Sun **13**	**Good for:** grand opening, fix house, wedding	*Snake*
Mon **14**	**Good for:** business, school *Bad for: grand opening, begin mission*	*Horse*

Tue **15**	⊖ **DON'T DO IMPORTANT THINGS** ⊖	*Sheep*
Wed **16**	**Good for:** business, contracts **Bad for:** *ground breaking, burial*	*Monkey*
Thu **17**	**Good for:** burial, ground breaking **Bad for:** *wedding, grand opening*	*Rooster*
Fri **18**	**Good for:** prayer **Bad for:** *grand opening, ground breaking*	*Dog*
Sat **19**	⊖ **DON'T DO IMPORTANT THINGS** ⊖	*Pig*
Sun **20**	**Good for:** grand opening, moving, wedding	*Rat*
Mon **21**	**Good for:** burial, ground breaking **Bad for:** *begin mission*	*Ox*
Tue **22**	⊖ **DON'T DO IMPORTANT THINGS** ⊖	*Tiger*
Wed **23**	⊖ **DON'T DO IMPORTANT THINGS** ⊖	*Rabbit*
Thu **24**	**Good for:** prayer, worship **Bad for:** *ground breaking, grand opening*	*Dragon*
Fri **25**	**Good for:** contracts, grand opening, wedding	*Snake*
Sat **26**	**Good for:** buy property, ground breaking, wedding	*Horse*
Sun **27**	⊖ **DON'T DO IMPORTANT THINGS** ⊖	*Sheep*
Mon **28**	**Good for:** prayer, business **Bad for:** *fix house, school*	*Monkey*

S	M	T	W	T	F	S
		1	2	3	4	5
6	7	8	9	10	11	12
13	14	15	16	17	18	19
20	21	22	23	24	25	26
27	28	29	30	31		

March 2011

Unfavorable for:

Day	Activities	Unfavorable for
Tue 1	**Good for:** ground breaking, business *Bad for: moving, travel*	*Rooster*
Wed 2	**Good for:** grand opening, ground breaking, wedding	*Dog*
Thu 3	⊖ **DON'T DO IMPORTANT THINGS** ⊖	*Pig*
Fri 4	**Good for:** grand opening, moving, wedding *Bad for: burial*	*Rat*
Sat 5	⊖ **DON'T DO IMPORTANT THINGS** ⊖	*Ox*
Sun 6	**Good for:** worship, prayer *Bad for: grand opening, ground breaking*	*Tiger*
Mon 7	⊖ **DON'T DO IMPORTANT THINGS** ⊖	*Rabbit*
Tue 8	**Good for:** planting, prayer *Bad for: wedding, burial*	*Dragon*
Wed 9	**Good for:** prayer, worship *Bad for: ground breaking, wedding*	*Snake*
Thu 10	**Good for:** prayer, worship *Bad for: grand opening, contracts*	*Horse*
Fri 11	**Good for:** grand opening, ground breaking, wedding	*Sheep*
Sat 12	**Good for:** burial, ground breaking *Bad for: wedding, grand opening*	*Monkey*
Sun 13	**Good for:** begin mission, moving *Bad for: burial, ground breaking*	*Rooster*
Mon 14	**Good for:** moving, prayer, worship *Bad for: ground breaking*	*Dog*
Tue 15	**Good for:** grand opening, contracts *Bad for: burial, lawsuit*	*Pig*

Day	Details	Zodiac
Wed **16**	**Good for:** prayer, worship *Bad for: grand opening, wedding*	Rat
Thu **17**	**Good for:** contracts, fix house, ground breaking *Bad for: wedding, lawsuit*	Ox
Fri **18**	**Good for:** prayer *Bad for: ground breaking*	Tiger
Sat **19**	⊖ **DON'T DO IMPORTANT THINGS** ⊖	Rabbit
Sun **20**	**Good for:** begin mission, school, grand opening	Dragon
Mon **21**	**Good for:** moving, school, ground breaking	Snake
Tue **22**	⊖ **DON'T DO IMPORTANT THINGS** ⊖	Horse
Wed **23**	**Good for:** grand opening, ground breaking, wedding	Sheep
Thu **24**	**Good for:** ground breaking, planting, burial *Bad for: wedding*	Monkey
Fri **25**	⊖ **DON'T DO IMPORTANT THINGS** ⊖	Rooster
Sat **26**	**Good for:** prayer *Bad for: grand opening, wedding*	Dog
Sun **27**	**Good for:** business, grand opening, contracts *Bad for: ground breaking, burial*	Pig
Mon **28**	**Good for:** prayer, worship *Bad for: burial, grand opening*	Rat
Tue **29**	**Good for:** fix house, moving, ground breaking *Bad for: begin mission, funeral*	Ox
Wed **30**	**Good for:** prayer, school *Bad for: ground breaking, lawsuit*	Tiger
Thu **31**	⊖ **DON'T DO IMPORTANT THINGS** ⊖	Rabbit

April 2011

Unfavorable for:

Fri **1**	**Good for:** prayer, worship ***Bad for:*** *ground breaking, grand opening, wedding*	*Dragon*
Sat **2**	⊖ **DON'T DO IMPORTANT THINGS** ⊖	*Snake*
Sun **3**	**Good for:** grand opening, ground breaking, wedding	*Horse*
Mon **4**	**Good for:** prayer, worship ***Bad for:*** *grand opening, wedding*	*Sheep*
Tue **5**	**Good for:** fix house, grand opening, wedding	*Monkey*
Wed **6**	⊖ **DON'T DO IMPORTANT THINGS** ⊖	*Rooster*
Thu **7**	**Good for:** prayer, worship ***Bad for:*** *business, grand opening, ground breaking*	*Dog*
Fri **8**	⊖ **DON'T DO IMPORTANT THINGS** ⊖	*Pig*
Sat **9**	**Good for:** business, prayer, worship ***Bad for:*** *burial, ground breaking*	*Rat*
Sun **10**	**Good for:** prayer, worship ***Bad for:*** *grand opening, wedding*	*Ox*
Mon **11**	**Good for:** burial, ground breaking, worship ***Bad for:*** *wedding*	*Tiger*
Tue **12**	**Good for:** business, contracts ***Bad for:*** *ground breaking, burial*	*Rabbit*
Wed **13**	**Good for:** prayer, worship ***Bad for:*** *wedding*	*Dragon*
Thu **14**	**Good for:** planting, school ***Bad for:*** *burial, ground breaking*	*Snake*
Fri **15**	**Good for:** grand opening, ground breaking, wedding	*Horse*

Sat **16**	**Good for:** prayer, worship *Bad for: grand opening, wedding*	*Sheep*
Sun **17**	**Good for:** business, grand opening, wedding *Bad for: burial, lawsuit*	*Monkey*
Mon **18**	⊜ **DON'T DO IMPORTANT THINGS** ⊜	*Rooster*
Tue **19**	**Good for:** prayer, worship *Bad for: ground breaking, moving*	*Dog*
Wed **20**	**Good for:** planting, worship, prayer *Bad for: lawsuit, travel*	*Pig*
Thu **21**	**Good for:** business, prayer, worship *Bad for: grand opening, wedding*	*Rat*
Fri **22**	**Good for:** business, contracts, school *Bad for: burial, ground breaking*	*Ox*
Sat **23**	**Good for:** prayer, worship *Bad for: wedding*	*Tiger*
Sun **24**	**Good for:** begin mission, grand opening, wedding *Bad for: burial, ground breaking*	*Rabbit*
Mon **25**	**Good for:** planting, prayer, worship *Bad for: grand opening, ground breaking*	*Dragon*
Tue **26**	**Good for:** planting, business, contracts *Bad for: lawsuit, travel*	*Snake*
Wed **27**	**Good for:** burial, grand opening, wedding	*Horse*
Thu **28**	**Good for:** prayer, worship *Bad for: grand opening, ground breaking*	*Sheep*
Fri **29**	**Good for:** fix house, wedding, ground breaking	*Monkey*
Sat **30**	⊜ **DON'T DO IMPORTANT THINGS** ⊜	*Rooster*

S	M	T	W	T	F	S
1	2	3	4	5	6	7
8	9	10	11	12	13	14
15	16	17	18	19	20	21
22	23	24	25	26	27	28
29	30	31				

May 2011

Unfavorable for:

Sun **1**	**Good for:** prayer, worship *Bad for:* *ground breaking, wedding*	*Dog*
Mon **2**	**Good for:** begin mission, contracts, grand opening *Bad for:* *lawsuit*	*Pig*
Tue **3**	**Good for:** planting, worship *Bad for:* *business, fix house, travel*	*Rat*
Wed **4**	**Good for:** prayer, worship *Bad for:* *grand opening, wedding*	*Ox*
Thu **5**	⊖ **DON'T DO IMPORTANT THINGS** ⊖	*Tiger*
Fri **6**	⊖ **DON'T DO IMPORTANT THINGS** ⊖	*Rabbit*
Sat **7**	⊖ **DON'T DO IMPORTANT THINGS** ⊖	*Dragon*
Sun **8**	⊖ **DON'T DO IMPORTANT THINGS** ⊖	*Snake*
Mon **9**	**Good for:** prayer, worship *Bad for:* *grand opening, ground breaking, wedding*	*Horse*
Tue **10**	**Good for:** grand opening, ground breaking, wedding	*Sheep*
Wed **11**	**Good for:** contracts, wedding, moving	*Monkey*
Thu **12**	**Good for:** prayer, school, worship *Bad for:* *wedding, grand opening*	*Rooster*
Fri **13**	⊖ **DON'T DO IMPORTANT THINGS** ⊖	*Dog*
Sat **14**	**Good for:** prayer, worship *Bad for:* *wedding, lawsuit*	*Pig*
Sun **15**	**Good for:** fix house, moving, wedding	*Rat*

Day		Activities	Zodiac
Mon **16**		**Good for:** burial, planting ***Bad for:*** *grand opening, wedding*	*Ox*
Tue **17**		**Good for:** prayer, worship ***Bad for:*** *grand opening, ground breaking*	*Tiger*
Wed **18**	⊖	**DON'T DO IMPORTANT THINGS** ⊖	*Rabbit*
Thu **19**		**Good for:** prayer, worship ***Bad for:*** *begin mission, grand opening, travel*	*Dragon*
Fri **20**	⊖	**DON'T DO IMPORTANT THINGS** ⊖	*Snake*
Sat **21**		**Good for:** begin mission, fix house, planting ***Bad for:*** *business, contracts*	*Horse*
Sun **22**		**Good for:** burial, grand opening, wedding	*Sheep*
Mon **23**	⊖	**DON'T DO IMPORTANT THINGS** ⊖	*Monkey*
Tue **24**		**Good for:** prayer, school, worship ***Bad for:*** *grand opening, wedding*	*Rooster*
Wed **25**		**Good for:** prayer, worship ***Bad for:*** *wedding, travel, lawsuit*	*Dog*
Thu **26**		**Good for:** contracts, moving, wedding ***Bad for:*** *burial, ground breaking*	*Pig*
Fri **27**		**Good for:** burial, ground breaking ***Bad for:*** *contracts, lawsuit*	*Rat*
Sat **28**		**Good for:** worship ***Bad for:*** *ground breaking, wedding*	*Ox*
Sun **29**		**Good for:** planting, prayer ***Bad for:*** *travel, wedding*	*Tiger*
Mon **30**	⊖	**DON'T DO IMPORTANT THINGS** ⊖	*Rabbit*
Tue **31**	⊖	**DON'T DO IMPORTANT THINGS** ⊖	*Dragon*

S	M	T	W	T	F	S
			1	2	3	4
5	6	7	8	9	10	11
12	13	14	15	16	17	18
19	20	21	22	23	24	25
26	27	28	29	30		

June 2011

Unfavorable for:

Day		Unfavorable for:
Wed 1	⊖ **DON'T DO IMPORTANT THINGS** ⊖	*Snake*
Thu 2	**Good for:** prayer, worship *Bad for: grand opening, wedding*	*Horse*
Fri 3	**Good for:** worship *Bad for: grand opening, ground breaking*	*Sheep*
Sat 4	**Good for:** business, contracts, grand opening	*Monkey*
Sun 5	**Good for:** prayer, worship *Bad for: grand opening, wedding, ground breaking*	*Rooster*
Mon 6	**Good for:** begin mission, contracts, travel *Bad for: funeral, lawsuit*	*Dog*
Tue 7	**Good for:** begin mission, school *Bad for: burial, ground breaking*	*Pig*
Wed 8	**Good for:** prayer, worship *Bad for: business, fix house, grand opening*	*Rat*
Thu 9	**Good for:** planting, prayer, worship *Bad for: grand opening, wedding*	*Ox*
Fri 10	**Good for:** grand opening, ground breaking, wedding	*Tiger*
Sat 11	⊖ **DON'T DO IMPORTANT THINGS** ⊖	*Rabbit*
Sun 12	**Good for:** fix house, grand opening, moving	*Dragon*
Mon 13	**Good for:** prayer, worship *Bad for: grand opening, ground breaking, wedding*	*Snake*
Tue 14	⊖ **DON'T DO IMPORTANT THINGS** ⊖	*Horse*
Wed 15	**Good for:** prayer, worship *Bad for: ground breaking, wedding*	*Sheep*

Thu	**16**	**Good for:** burial, buy property, travel *Bad for: lawsuit*	*Monkey*
Fri	**17**	**Good for:** prayer, worship *Bad for: business, buy property, wedding*	*Rooster*
Sat	**18**	**Good for:** planting, prayer *Bad for: grand opening, wedding*	*Dog*
Sun	**19**	**Good for:** moving, wedding, begin mission *Bad for: ground breaking*	*Pig*
Mon	**20**	**Good for:** worship, prayer *Bad for: ground breaking, wedding*	*Rat*
Tue	**21**	● **DON'T DO IMPORTANT THINGS** ●	*Ox*
Wed	**22**	**Good for:** worship, prayer *Bad for: ground breaking, grand opening*	*Tiger*
Thu	**23**	● **DON'T DO IMPORTANT THINGS** ●	*Rabbit*
Fri	**24**	**Good for:** begin mission, business, contracts *Bad for: burial, funeral*	*Dragon*
Sat	**25**	**Good for:** worship, prayer *Bad for: grand opening, ground breaking*	*Snake*
Sun	**26**	● **DON'T DO IMPORTANT THINGS** ●	*Horse*
Mon	**27**	**Good for:** worship *Bad for: grand opening, wedding*	*Sheep*
Tue	**28**	**Good for:** grand opening, ground breaking, wedding	*Monkey*
Wed	**29**	**Good for:** prayer, worship *Bad for: burial, ground breaking, wedding*	*Rooster*
Thu	**30**	**Good for:** begin mission, fix house, grand opening	*Dog*

S	M	T	W	T	F	S
					1	2
3	4	5	6	7	8	9
10	11	12	13	14	15	16
17	18	19	20	21	22	23
24	25	26	27	28	29	30
31						

July 2011

Unfavorable for:

Day		Unfavorable
Fri **1**	● **DON'T DO IMPORTANT THINGS** ●	*Pig*
Sat **2**	**Good for:** worship ***Bad for:*** *grand opening, wedding, ground breaking*	*Rat*
Sun **3**	**Good for:** grand opening, school, wedding	*Ox*
Mon **4**	**Good for:** begin mission, business, contracts ***Bad for:*** *ground breaking, lawsuit*	*Tiger*
Tue **5**	● **DON'T DO IMPORTANT THINGS** ●	*Rabbit*
Wed **6**	**Good for:** grand opening, ground breaking, wedding	*Dragon*
Thu **7**	**Good for:** prayer, worship ***Bad for:*** *grand opening, wedding*	*Snake*
Fri **8**	**Good for:** ground breaking, wedding, buy property	*Horse*
Sat **9**	● **DON'T DO IMPORTANT THINGS** ●	*Sheep*
Sun **10**	**Good for:** begin mission, fix house, grand opening	*Monkey*
Mon **11**	**Good for:** business, grand opening, wedding	*Rooster*
Tue **12**	**Good for:** worship ***Bad for:*** *burial, ground breaking, wedding*	*Dog*
Wed **13**	**Good for:** begin mission, school ***Bad for:*** *ground breaking, lawsuit*	*Pig*
Thu **14**	**Good for:** burial, ground breaking, worship ***Bad for:*** *wedding, grand opening*	*Rat*
Fri **15**	**Good for:** contracts, moving, travel ***Bad for:*** *grand opening, ground breaking*	*Ox*

Sat	16	**Good for:** worship *Bad for: contracts, grand opening, wedding*	*Tiger*
Sun	17	⊖ **DON'T DO IMPORTANT THINGS** ⊖	*Rabbit*
Mon	18	**Good for:** prayer, worship *Bad for: fix house, ground breaking, moving*	*Dragon*
Tue	19	**Good for:** business, fix house, moving *Bad for: ground breaking, lawsuit*	*Snake*
Wed	20	⊖ **DON'T DO IMPORTANT THINGS** ⊖	*Horse*
Thu	21	⊖ **DON'T DO IMPORTANT THINGS** ⊖	*Sheep*
Fri	22	**Good for:** contracts, grand opening, ground breaking *Bad for: wedding, fix house*	*Monkey*
Sat	23	**Good for:** fix house, travel, wedding	*Rooster*
Sun	24	⊖ **DON'T DO IMPORTANT THINGS** ⊖	*Dog*
Mon	25	**Good for:** begin mission, school *Bad for: ground breaking, moving*	*Pig*
Tue	26	**Good for:** worship, ground breaking, burial *Bad for: begin mission, lawsuit*	*Rat*
Wed	27	**Good for:** begin mission, moving, planting *Bad for: buy property, fix house, grand opening*	*Ox*
Thu	28	**Good for:** fix house, ground breaking, wedding	*Tiger*
Fri	29	**Good for:** worship *Bad for: grand opening, wedding*	*Rabbit*
Sat	30	⊖ **DON'T DO IMPORTANT THINGS** ⊖	*Dragon*
Sun	31	**Good for:** business, contracts, moving *Bad for: fix house, ground breaking*	*Snake*

S	M	T	W	T	F	S
	1	2	3	4	5	6
7	8	9	10	11	12	13
14	15	16	17	18	19	20
21	22	23	24	25	26	27
28	29	30	31			

August 2011

Unfavorable for:

Day	Details	Unfavorable for
Mon 1	**Good for:** begin mission, grand opening, wedding	*Horse*
Tue 2	⊜ **DON'T DO IMPORTANT THINGS** ⊜	*Sheep*
Wed 3	**Good for:** begin mission, contracts, grand opening *Bad for: ground breaking, burial*	*Monkey*
Thu 4	**Good for:** grand opening, ground breaking, wedding	*Rooster*
Fri 5	**Good for:** planting, worship *Bad for: grand opening, wedding*	*Dog*
Sat 6	**Good for:** begin mission, school *Bad for: burial, lawsuit*	*Pig*
Sun 7	**Good for:** burial, ground breaking, worship *Bad for: grand opening, wedding*	*Rat*
Mon 8	⊜ **DON'T DO IMPORTANT THINGS** ⊜	*Ox*
Tue 9	**Good for:** prayer, worship *Bad for: ground breaking, grand opening*	*Tiger*
Wed 10	⊜ **DON'T DO IMPORTANT THINGS** ⊜	*Rabbit*
Thu 11	**Good for:** begin mission, grand opening, wedding	*Dragon*
Fri 12	**Good for:** prayer, worship *Bad for: grand opening, wedding*	*Snake*
Sat 13	**Good for:** contracts, grand opening, wedding	*Horse*
Sun 14	⊜ **DON'T DO IMPORTANT THINGS** ⊜	*Sheep*
Mon 15	⊜ **DON'T DO IMPORTANT THINGS** ⊜	*Monkey*

Tue	**16**	**Good for:** contracts, moving, wedding *Bad for: burial, ground breaking*	*Rooster*
Wed	**17**	**Good for:** prayer, worship *Bad for: grand opening, wedding*	*Dog*
Thu	**18**	**Good for:** worship *Bad for: burial, funeral, wedding*	*Pig*
Fri	**19**	**Good for:** school, worship *Bad for: fix house, ground breaking*	*Rat*
Sat	**20**	**Good for:** worship *Bad for: grand opening, wedding*	*Ox*
Sun	**21**	**Good for:** grand opening, ground breaking, wedding	*Tiger*
Mon	**22**	⊖ **DON'T DO IMPORTANT THINGS** ⊖	*Rabbit*
Tue	**23**	**Good for:** prayer, worship, planting *Bad for: contracts, wedding*	*Dragon*
Wed	**24**	**Good for:** prayer, worship *Bad for: grand opening, ground breaking*	*Snake*
Thu	**25**	**Good for:** begin mission, grand opening, wedding	*Horse*
Fri	**26**	**Good for:** burial, fix house, ground breaking *Bad for: contracts, wedding*	*Sheep*
Sat	**27**	⊖ **DON'T DO IMPORTANT THINGS** ⊖	*Monkey*
Sun	**28**	⊖ **DON'T DO IMPORTANT THINGS** ⊖	*Rooster*
Mon	**29**	**Good for:** begin mission, school, worship *Bad for: contracts, grand opening*	*Dog*
Tue	**30**	**Good for:** grand opening, moving, wedding	*Pig*
Wed	**31**	**Good for:** contracts, wedding, begin mission *Bad for: ground breaking, lawsuit*	*Rat*

S	M	T	W	T	F	S
				1	2	3
4	5	6	7	8	9	10
11	12	13	14	15	16	17
18	19	20	21	22	23	24
25	26	27	28	29	30	

September 2011

Unfavorable for:

Day		Unfavorable for:
Thu 1	⊝ **DON'T DO IMPORTANT THINGS** ⊝	*Ox*
Fri 2	**Good for:** begin mission, prayer, worship ***Bad for:*** *ground breaking, wedding*	*Tiger*
Sat 3	⊝ **DON'T DO IMPORTANT THINGS** ⊝	*Rabbit*
Sun 4	**Good for:** grand opening, ground breaking, wedding	*Dragon*
Mon 5	⊝ **DON'T DO IMPORTANT THINGS** ⊝	*Snake*
Tue 6	**Good for:** contracts, wedding, ground breaking	*Horse*
Wed 7	**Good for:** planting, school ***Bad for:*** *fix house, ground breaking*	*Sheep*
Thu 8	⊝ **DON'T DO IMPORTANT THINGS** ⊝	*Monkey*
Fri 9	⊝ **DON'T DO IMPORTANT THINGS** ⊝	*Rooster*
Sat 10	**Good for:** prayer, worship ***Bad for:*** *grand opening, ground breaking, wedding*	*Dog*
Sun 11	**Good for:** contracts, grand opening, wedding	*Pig*
Mon 12	**Good for:** business, planting, worship ***Bad for:*** *fix house, moving*	*Rat*
Tue 13	**Good for:** contracts, school, wedding	*Ox*
Wed 14	**Good for:** worship ***Bad for:*** *grand opening, ground breaking, wedding*	*Tiger*
Thu 15	⊝ **DON'T DO IMPORTANT THINGS** ⊝	*Rabbit*

Fri **16**	**Good for:** begin mission, business *Bad for: burial, ground breaking*	*Dragon*
Sat **17**	**Good for:** grand opening, moving, wedding	*Snake*
Sun **18**	**Good for:** worship *Bad for: grand opening, wedding*	*Horse*
Mon **19**	**Good for:** grand opening, ground breaking, wedding	*Sheep*
Tue **20**	**Good for:** prayer, worship *Bad for: contracts, grand opening, ground breaking*	*Monkey*
Wed **21**	⊖ **DON'T DO IMPORTANT THINGS** ⊖	*Rooster*
Thu **22**	⊖ **DON'T DO IMPORTANT THINGS** ⊖	*Dog*
Fri **23**	**Good for:** fix house, grand opening, wedding	*Pig*
Sat **24**	**Good for:** prayer, worship *Bad for: contracts, grand opening, fix house*	*Rat*
Sun **25**	**Good for:** business, contracts, wedding	*Ox*
Mon **26**	**Good for:** contracts, burial, ground breaking *Bad for: grand opening, wedding*	*Tiger*
Tue **27**	⊖ **DON'T DO IMPORTANT THINGS** ⊖	*Rabbit*
Wed **28**	**Good for:** begin mission, business, planting *Bad for: grand opening, lawsuit*	*Dragon*
Thu **29**	**Good for:** grand opening, moving, school *Bad for: burial, ground breaking*	*Snake*
Fri **30**	**Good for:** worship *Bad for: grand opening, ground breaking, wedding*	*Horse*

S	M	T	W	T	F	S
						1
2	3	4	5	6	7	8
9	10	11	12	13	14	15
16	17	18	19	20	21	22
23	24	25	26	27	28	29
30	31					

October 2011

Unfavorable for:

Day		Unfavorable for:
Sat 1	⊖ **DON'T DO IMPORTANT THINGS** ⊖	*Sheep*
Sun 2	**Good for:** prayer, worship *Bad for: contracts, wedding*	*Monkey*
Mon 3	⊖ **DON'T DO IMPORTANT THINGS** ⊖	*Rooster*
Tue 4	**Good for:** worship *Bad for: grand opening, ground breaking, wedding*	*Dog*
Wed 5	**Good for:** grand opening, ground breaking, wedding	*Pig*
Thu 6	**Good for:** prayer, worship *Bad for: contracts, fix house, begin mission*	*Rat*
Fri 7	**Good for:** begin mission, grand opening, wedding	*Ox*
Sat 8	**Good for:** begin mission, grand opening, moving	*Tiger*
Sun 9	⊖ **DON'T DO IMPORTANT THINGS** ⊖	*Rabbit*
Mon 10	⊖ **DON'T DO IMPORTANT THINGS** ⊖	*Dragon*
Tue 11	**Good for:** prayer, worship *Bad for: grand opening, wedding, ground breaking*	*Snake*
Wed 12	**Good for:** worship *Bad for: contracts, lawsuit, travel*	*Horse*
Thu 13	**Good for:** prayer, worship *Bad for: grand opening, ground breaking, begin mission*	*Sheep*
Fri 14	⊖ **DON'T DO IMPORTANT THINGS** ⊖	*Monkey*
Sat 15	**Good for:** contracts, ground breaking, wedding	*Rooster*

Sun 16	🌑 **DON'T DO IMPORTANT THINGS** 🌑	*Dog*
Mon 17	**Good for:** prayer, planting, worship *Bad for: contracts, wedding, ground breaking*	*Pig*
Tue 18	**Good for:** grand opening, ground breaking, wedding	*Rat*
Wed 19	🌑 **DON'T DO IMPORTANT THINGS** 🌑	*Ox*
Thu 20	**Good for:** contracts, grand opening, wedding	*Tiger*
Fri 21	🌑 **DON'T DO IMPORTANT THINGS** 🌑	*Rabbit*
Sat 22	**Good for:** begin mission, moving, worship *Bad for: ground breaking, wedding*	*Dragon*
Sun 23	**Good for:** begin mission, worship *Bad for: grand opening, wedding*	*Snake*
Mon 24	**Good for:** worship *Bad for: contracts, ground breaking, travel*	*Horse*
Tue 25	🌑 **DON'T DO IMPORTANT THINGS** 🌑	*Sheep*
Wed 26	**Good for:** prayer, worship *Bad for: wedding, contracts*	*Monkey*
Thu 27	**Good for:** worship *Bad for: business, burial*	*Rooster*
Fri 28	🌑 **DON'T DO IMPORTANT THINGS** 🌑	*Dog*
Sat 29	**Good for:** worship, prayer *Bad for: grand opening, ground breaking*	*Pig*
Sun 30	**Good for:** school, grand opening, wedding	*Rat*
Mon 31	🌑 **DON'T DO IMPORTANT THINGS** 🌑	*Ox*

S	M	T	W	T	F	S
		1	2	3	4	5
6	7	8	9	10	11	12
13	14	15	16	17	18	19
20	21	22	23	24	25	26
27	28	29	30			

November 2011

Unfavorable for:

Date		Unfavorable for
Tue 1	**Good for:** moving, fix house, burial *Bad for: business, wedding*	*Tiger*
Wed 2	⊖ **DON'T DO IMPORTANT THINGS** ⊖	*Rabbit*
Thu 3	**Good for:** fix house, moving, ground breaking *Bad for: contracts, wedding*	*Dragon*
Fri 4	**Good for:** worship *Bad for: grand opening, ground breaking, wedding*	*Snake*
Sat 5	**Good for:** prayer, worship *Bad for: fix house, ground breaking, grand opening*	*Horse*
Sun 6	**Good for:** prayer *Bad for: grand opening, wedding, lawsuit*	*Sheep*
Mon 7	⊖ **DON'T DO IMPORTANT THINGS** ⊖	*Monkey*
Tue 8	**Good for:** grand opening, ground breaking, wedding	*Rooster*
Wed 9	**Good for:** worship *Bad for: contracts, wedding, grand opening*	*Dog*
Thu 10	⊖ **DON'T DO IMPORTANT THINGS** ⊖	*Pig*
Fri 11	**Good for:** grand opening, moving, wedding	*Rat*
Sat 12	**Good for:** contracts, grand opening, business	*Ox*
Sun 13	**Good for:** prayer, worship *Bad for: grand opening, ground breaking, wedding*	*Tiger*
Mon 14	⊖ **DON'T DO IMPORTANT THINGS** ⊖	*Rabbit*
Tue 15	**Good for:** prayer, worship *Bad for: contracts, ground breaking*	*Dragon*

108

Wed **16**	**Good for:** prayer, worship *Bad for: grand opening, wedding*	*Snake*
Thu **17**	**Good for:** begin mission, moving, school *Bad for: burial, ground breaking*	*Horse*
Fri **18**	**Good for:** worship *Bad for: contracts, grand opening, wedding*	*Sheep*
Sat **19**	**Good for:** grand opening, wedding, contracts *Bad for: ground breaking*	*Monkey*
Sun **20**	**Good for:** grand opening, ground breaking, wedding	*Rooster*
Mon **21**	**Good for:** begin mission, grand opening, wedding	*Dog*
Tue **22**	⬤ **DON'T DO IMPORTANT THINGS** ⬤	*Pig*
Wed **23**	**Good for:** worship *Bad for: contracts, grand opening, wedding*	*Rat*
Thu **24**	**Good for:** begin mission, grand opening, school *Bad for: ground breaking, burial*	*Ox*
Fri **25**	**Good for:** grand opening, ground breaking, wedding	*Tiger*
Sat **26**	⬤ **DON'T DO IMPORTANT THINGS** ⬤	*Rabbit*
Sun **27**	⬤ **DON'T DO IMPORTANT THINGS** ⬤	*Dragon*
Mon **28**	**Good for:** planting, prayer, worship *Bad for: contracts, wedding*	*Snake*
Tue **29**	⬤ **DON'T DO IMPORTANT THINGS** ⬤	*Horse*
Wed **30**	**Good for:** worship *Bad for: grand opening, wedding*	*Sheep*

S	M	T	W	T	F	S
				1	2	3
4	5	6	7	8	9	10
11	12	13	14	15	16	17
18	19	20	21	22	23	24
25	26	27	28	29	30	31

December 2011

Unfavorable for:

Thu 1	**Good for:** contracts, grand opening, wedding	*Monkey*
Fri 2	**Good for:** grand opening, ground breaking, wedding	*Rooster*
Sat 3	**Good for:** worship *Bad for: grand opening, ground breaking*	*Dog*
Sun 4	⊖ **DON'T DO IMPORTANT THINGS** ⊖	*Pig*
Mon 5	**Good for:** grand opening, moving, wedding ·	*Rat*
Tue 6	**Good for:** begin mission, grand opening, business *Bad for: burial, ground breaking*	*Ox*
Wed 7	**Good for:** prayer, worship *Bad for: contracts, grand opening, wedding*	*Tiger*
Thu 8	⊖ **DON'T DO IMPORTANT THINGS** ⊖	*Rabbit*
Fri 9	**Good for:** prayer, worship *Bad for: burial, ground breaking, fix house*	*Dragon*
Sat 10	⊖ **DON'T DO IMPORTANT THINGS** ⊖	*Snake*
Sun 11	**Good for:** worship *Bad for: buy property, fix house, moving*	*Horse*
Mon 12	**Good for:** contracts, wedding, ground breaking *Bad for: lawsuit*	*Sheep*
Tue 13	**Good for:** grand opening, ground breaking, wedding	*Monkey*
Wed 14	⊖ **DON'T DO IMPORTANT THINGS** ⊖	*Rooster*
Thu 15	**Good for:** contracts, grand opening, wedding	*Dog*

Fri **16**	**Good for:** burial, ground breaking, worship *Bad for: grand opening, wedding*	*Pig*
Sat **17**	⊖ **DON'T DO IMPORTANT THINGS** ⊖	*Rat*
Sun **18**	**Good for:** prayer, worship *Bad for: grand opening, ground breaking*	*Ox*
Mon **19**	**Good for:** business, grand opening, wedding	*Tiger*
Tue **20**	⊖ **DON'T DO IMPORTANT THINGS** ⊖	*Rabbit*
Wed **21**	**Good for:** fix house, ground breaking, school *Bad for: moving, travel*	*Dragon*
Thu **22**	⊖ **DON'T DO IMPORTANT THINGS** ⊖	*Snake*
Fri **23**	**Good for:** worship *Bad for: grand opening, ground breaking*	*Horse*
Sat **24**	**Good for:** grand opening, moving, wedding	*Sheep*
Sun **25**	**Good for:** begin mission, contracts, grand opening *Bad for: burial, ground breaking*	*Monkey*
Mon **26**	**Good for:** prayer, worship *Bad for: grand opening, contracts, wedding*	*Rooster*
Tue **27**	**Good for:** grand opening, school, wedding	*Dog*
Wed **28**	**Good for:** prayer, worship *Bad for: ground breaking, lawsuit*	*Pig*
Thu **29**	⊖ **DON'T DO IMPORTANT THINGS** ⊖	*Rat*
Fri **30**	**Good for:** Worship *Bad for: grand opening, wedding*	*Ox*
Sat **31**	**Good for:** contracts, grand opening, business *Bad for: burial, ground breaking*	*Tiger*

S	M	T	W	T	F	S
1	2	3	4	5	6	7
8	9	10	11	12	13	14
15	16	17	18	19	20	21
22	23	24	25	26	27	28
29	30	31				

January 2012

Unfavorable for:

Sun **1**	⊜ **DON'T DO IMPORTANT THINGS** ⊜	*Rabbit*
Mon **2**	**Good for:** grand opening, school, fix house *Bad for: ground breaking, lawsuit*	*Dragon*
Tue **3**	⊜ **DON'T DO IMPORTANT THINGS** ⊜	*Snake*
Wed **4**	**Good for:** prayer, planting, worship *Bad for: grand opening, wedding*	*Horse*
Thu **5**	**Good for:** grand opening, ground breaking, wedding	*Sheep*
Fri **6**	⊜ **DON'T DO IMPORTANT THINGS** ⊜	*Monkey*
Sat **7**	**Good for:** prayer, worship *Bad for: grand opening, ground breaking, wedding*	*Rooster*
Sun **8**	**Good for:** worship *Bad for: contracts, burial, begin mission*	*Dog*
Mon **9**	**Good for:** contracts, fix house, wedding	*Pig*
Tue **10**	**Good for:** grand opening, ground breaking, wedding	*Rat*
Wed **11**	⊜ **DON'T DO IMPORTANT THINGS** ⊜	*Ox*
Thu **12**	**Good for:** worship *Bad for: grand opening, lawsuit, wedding*	*Tiger*
Fri **13**	⊜ **DON'T DO IMPORTANT THINGS** ⊜	*Rabbit*
Sat **14**	**Good for:** prayer, worship *Bad for: contracts, grand opening, moving*	*Dragon*
Sun **15**	**Good for:** fix house, grand opening, ground breaking *Bad for: lawsuit*	*Snake*

Mon **16**	**Good for:** burial, worship *Bad for: moving, ground breaking*	*Horse*
Tue **17**	⊖ **DON'T DO IMPORTANT THINGS** ⊖	*Sheep*
Wed **18**	**Good for:** worship *Bad for: grand opening, wedding, ground breaking*	*Monkey*
Thu **19**	**Good for:** prayer, worship *Bad for: burial, ground breaking*	*Rooster*
Fri **20**	**Good for:** prayer, worship *Bad for: contracts, wedding*	*Dog*
Sat **21**	**Good for:** business, contracts, fix house *Bad for: grand opening, wedding*	*Pig*
Sun **22**	**Good for:** worship *Bad for: moving, travel, wedding*	*Rat*
Mon **23**	⊖ **DON'T DO IMPORTANT THINGS** ⊖	*Ox*
Tue **24**	**Good for:** burial, grand opening, ground breaking *Bad for: contracts, lawsuit*	*Tiger*
Wed **25**	⊖ **DON'T DO IMPORTANT THINGS** ⊖	*Rabbit*
Thu **26**	**Good for:** planting, prayer, worship *Bad for: grand opening, wedding*	*Dragon*
Fri **27**	**Good for:** worship *Bad for: business, contracts, wedding*	*Snake*
Sat **28**	**Good for:** prayer, worship *Bad for: begin mission, grand opening, ground breaking*	*Horse*
Sun **29**	⊖ **DON'T DO IMPORTANT THINGS** ⊖	*Sheep*
Mon **30**	**Good for:** grand opening, ground breaking, wedding	*Monkey*
Tue **31**	**Good for:** planting, prayer, worship *Bad for: contracts, grand opening, wedding*	*Rooster*

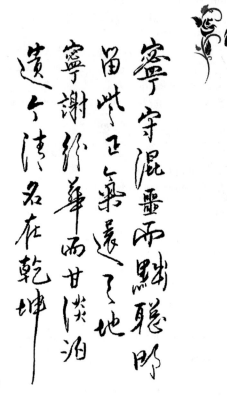

寧守混噩而黜聰明
留些正氣還天地
寧謝紛華而甘淡泊
遺個清名在乾坤

曾希書

It is preferable to be a little less witty and
stay away from shrewdness, in order to
reserve some righteousness for the world.

It is preferable to be rid of extravagance
and lead a simple life, in order to reserve
an uncontaminated name in history.

Ten Thousand Year Calendar

Ten-Thousand Year Calendar

	1ST MONTH Geng Yin	2ND MONTH Xin Mao	3RD MONTH Ren Chen	4TH MONTH Gui Si	5TH MONTH Jia Wu	6TH MONTH Yi Wei	
1	2/3 Ji Chou	3/5 Ji Wei	4/3 Wu Zi	5/3 Wu Wu	6/2 Wu Zi	7/1 Ding Si	1
2	2/4 Geng Yin	3/6 Geng Shen	4/4 Ji Chou	5/4 Ji Wei	6/3 Ji Chou	7/2 Wu Wu	2
3	2/5 Xin Mao	3/7 Xin You	4/5 Geng Yin	5/5 Geng Shen	6/4 Geng Yin	7/3 Ji Wei	3
4	2/6 Ren Chen	3/8 Ren Xu	4/6 Xin Mao	5/6 Xin You	6/5 Xin Mao	7/4 Geng Shen	4
5	2/7 Gui Si	3/9 Gui Hai	4/7 Ren Chen	5/7 Ren Xu	6/6 Ren Chen	7/5 Xin You	5
6	2/8 Jia Wu	3/10 Jia Zi	4/8 Gui Si	5/8 Gui Hai	6/7 Gui Si	7/6 Ren Xu	6
7	2/9 Yi Wei	3/11 Yi Chou	4/9 Jia Wu	5/9 Jia Zi	6/8 Jia Wu	7/7 Gui Hai	7
8	2/10 Bing Shen	3/12 Bing Yin	4/10 Yi Wei	5/10 Yi Chou	6/9 Yi Wei	7/8 Jia Zi	8
9	2/11 Ding You	3/13 Ding Mao	4/11 Bing Shen	5/11 Bing Yin	6/10 Bing Shen	7/9 Yi Chou	9
10	2/12 Wu Xu	3/14 Wu Chen	4/12 Ding You	5/12 Ding Mao	6/11 Ding You	7/10 Bing Yin	10
11	2/13 Ji Hai	3/15 Ji Si	4/13 Wu Xu	5/13 Wu Chen	6/12 Wu Xu	7/11 Ding Mao	11
12	2/14 Geng Zi	3/16 Geng Wu	4/14 Ji Hai	5/14 Ji Si	6/13 Ji Hai	7/12 Wu Chen	12
13	2/15 Xin Chou	3/17 Xin Wei	4/15 Geng Zi	5/15 Geng Wu	6/14 Geng Zi	7/13 Ji Si	13
14	2/16 Ren Yin	3/18 Ren Shen	4/16 Xin Chou	5/16 Xin Wei	6/15 Xin Chou	7/14 Geng Wu	14
15	2/17 Gui Mao	3/19 Gui You	4/17 Ren Yin	5/17 Ren Shen	6/16 Ren Yin	7/15 Xin Wei	15
16	2/18 Jia Chen	3/20 Jia Xu	4/18 Gui Mao	5/18 Gui You	6/17 Gui Mao	7/16 Ren Shen	16
17	2/19 Yi Si	3/21 Yi Hai	4/19 Jia Chen	5/19 Jia Xu	6/18 Jia Chen	7/17 Gui You	17
18	2/20 Bing Wu	3/22 Bing Zi	4/20 Yi Si	5/20 Yi Hai	6/19 Yi Si	7/18 Jia Xu	18
19	2/21 Ding Wei	3/23 Ding Chou	4/21 Bing Wu	5/21 Bing Zi	6/20 Bing Wu	7/19 Yi Hai	19
20	2/22 Wu Shen	3/24 Wu Yin	4/22 Ding Wei	5/22 Ding Chou	6/21 Ding Wei	7/20 Bing Zi	20
21	2/23 Ji You	3/25 Ji Mao	4/23 Wu Shen	5/23 Wu Yin	6/22 Wu Shen	7/21 Ding Chou	21
22	2/24 Geng Xu	3/26 Geng Chen	4/24 Ji You	5/24 Ji Mao	6/23 Ji You	7/22 Wu Yin	22
23	2/25 Xin Hai	3/27 Xin Si	4/25 Geng Xu	5/25 Geng Chen	6/24 Geng Xu	7/23 Ji Mao	23
24	2/26 Ren Zi	3/28 Ren Wu	4/26 Xin Hai	5/26 Xin Si	6/25 Xin Hai	7/24 Geng Chen	24
25	2/27 Gui Chou	3/29 Gui Wei	4/27 Ren Zi	5/27 Ren Wu	6/26 Ren Zi	7/25 Xin Si	25
26	2/28 Jia Yin	3/30 Jia Shen	4/28 Gui Chou	5/28 Gui Wei	6/27 Gui Chou	7/26 Ren Wu	26
27	3/1 Yi Mao	3/31 Yi You	4/29 Jia Yin	5/29 Jia Shen	6/28 Jia Yin	7/27 Gui Wei	27
28	3/2 Bing Chen	4/1 Bing Xu	4/30 Yi Mao	5/30 Yi You	6/29 Yi Mao	7/28 Jia Shen	28
29	3/3 Ding Si	4/2 Ding Hai	5/1 Bing Chen	5/31 Bing Xu	6/30 Bing Chen	7/29 Yi You	29
30	3/4 Wu Wu		5/2 Ding Si	6/1 Ding Hai		7/30 Bing Xu	30
	8 White	7 Red	6 White	5 Yellow	4 Green	3 Jade	
Jie	Li Chun 2/4 12:32pm	Jing Zhi 3/6 6:43am	Qing Ming 4/5 11:46am	Li Xia 5/6 5:20am	Mang Zhong 6/6 9:43am	Xiao Shu 7/7 8:06pm	Jie
Qi	Yu Shui 2/19 8:24am	Chun Fen 3/21 7:37am	Gu Yu 4/20 6:56pm	Xiao Man 5/21 6:18pm	Xia Zhi 6/22 2:24am	Da Shu 7/23 1:17pm	Qi

 2011

Year: Xin Mao · 7 Red

	7TH MONTH Bing Shen	8TH MONTH Ding You	9TH MONTH Wu Xu	10TH MONTH Ji Hai	11TH MONTH Geng Zi	12TH MONTH Xin Chou	
						2011 - 2012	
1	7/31 Ding Hai	8/29 Bing Chen	9/27 Yi You	10/27 Yi Mao	11/25 Jia Shen	12/25 Jia Yin	1
2	8/1 Wu Zi	8/30 Ding Si	9/28 Bing Xu	10/28 Bing Chen	11/26 Yi You	12/26 Yi Mao	2
3	8/2 Ji Chou	8/31 Wu Wu	9/29 Ding Hai	10/29 Ding Si	11/27 Bing Xu	12/27 Bing Chen	3
4	8/3 Geng Yin	9/1 Ji Wei	9/30 Wu Zi	10/30 Wu Wu	11/28 Ding Hai	12/28 Ding Si	4
5	8/4 Xin Mao	9/2 Geng Shen	10/1 Ji Chou	10/31 Ji Wei	11/29 Wu Zi	12/29 Wu Wu	5
6	8/5 Ren Chen	9/3 Xin You	10/2 Geng Yin	11/1 Geng Shen	11/30 Ji Chou	12/30 Ji Wei	6
7	8/6 Gui Si	9/4 Ren Xu	10/3 Xin Mao	11/2 Xin You	12/1 Geng Yin	12/31 Geng Shen	7
8	8/7 Jia Wu	9/5 Gui Hai	10/4 Ren Chen	11/3 Ren Xu	12/2 Xin Mao	1/1 Xin You	8
9	8/8 Yi Wei	9/6 Jia Zi	10/5 Gui Si	11/4 Gui Hai	12/3 Ren Chen	1/2 Ren Xu	9
10	8/9 Bing Shen	9/7 Yi Chou	10/6 Jia Wu	11/5 Jia Zi	12/4 Gui Si	1/3 Gui Hai	10
11	8/10 Ding You	9/8 Bing Yin	10/7 Yi Wei	11/6 Yi Chou	12/5 Jia Wu	1/4 Jia Zi	11
12	8/11 Wu Xu	9/9 Ding Mao	10/8 Bing Shen	11/7 Bing Yin	12/6 Yi Wei	1/5 Yi Chou	12
13	8/12 Ji Hai	9/10 Wu Chen	10/9 Ding You	11/8 Ding Mao	12/7 Bing Shen	1/6 Bing Yin	13
14	8/13 Geng Zi	9/11 Ji Si	10/10 Wu Xu	11/9 Wu Chen	12/8 Ding You	1/7 Ding Mao	14
15	8/14 Xin Chou	9/12 Geng Wu	10/11 Ji Hai	11/10 Ji Si	12/9 Wu Xu	1/8 Wu Chen	15
16	8/15 Ren Yin	9/13 Xin Wei	10/12 Geng Zi	11/11 Geng Wu	12/10 Ji Hai	1/9 Ji Si	16
17	8/16 Gui Mao	9/14 Ren Shen	10/13 Xin Chou	11/12 Xin Wei	12/11 Geng Zi	1/10 Geng Wu	17
18	8/17 Jia Chen	9/15 Gui You	10/14 Ren Yin	11/13 Ren Shen	12/12 Xin Chou	1/11 Xin Wei	18
19	8/18 Yi Si	9/16 Jia Xu	10/15 Gui Mao	11/14 Gui You	12/13 Ren Yin	1/12 Ren Shen	19
20	8/19 Bing Wu	9/17 Yi Hai	10/16 Jia Chen	11/15 Jia Xu	12/14 Gui Mao	1/13 Gui You	20
21	8/20 Ding Wei	9/18 Bing Zi	10/17 Yi Si	11/16 Yi Hai	12/15 Jia Chen	1/14 Jia Xu	21
22	8/21 Wu Shen	9/19 Ding Chou	10/18 Bing Wu	11/17 Bing Zi	12/16 Yi Si	1/15 Yi Hai	22
23	8/22 Ji You	9/20 Wu Yin	10/19 Ding Wei	11/18 Ding Chou	12/17 Bing Wu	1/16 Bing Zi	23
24	8/23 Geng Xu	9/21 Ji Mao	10/20 Wu Shen	11/19 Wu Yin	12/18 Ding Wei	1/17 Ding Chou	24
25	8/24 Xin Hai	9/22 Geng Chen	10/21 Ji You	11/20 Ji Mao	12/19 Wu Shen	1/18 Wu Yin	25
26	8/25 Ren Zi	9/23 Xin Si	10/22 Geng Xu	11/21 Geng Chen	12/20 Ji You	1/19 Ji Mao	26
27	8/26 Gui Chou	9/24 Ren Wu	10/23 Xin Hai	11/22 Xin Si	12/21 Geng Xu	1/20 Geng Chen	27
28	8/27 Jia Yin	9/25 Gui Wei	10/24 Ren Zi	11/23 Ren Wu	12/22 Xin Hai	1/21 Xin Si	28
29	8/28 Yi Mao	9/26 Jia Shen	10/25 Gui Chou	11/24 Gui Wei	12/23 Ren Zi	1/22 Ren Wu	29
30			10/26 Jia Yin		12/24 Gui Chou		30
	2 Black	1 White	9 Purple	8 White	7 Red	6 White	
Jie	Li Qiu 8/8 5:49am	Bai Lu 9/8 8:33am	Han Lu 10/8 11:57pm	Li Dong 11/8 2:52am	Da Xue 12/7 7:32pm	Xiao Han 1/6 6:41am	Jie
Qi	Chu Shu 8/23 8:13pm	Qiu Fen 9/23 5:37pm	Shuang Jiang 10/24 2:43am	Xiao Xue 11/23 12:05am	Dong Zhi 12/22 1:18pm	Da Han 1/20 11:56pm	Qi

AFSI Book Store

The Principles of Feng Shui - Book One

After years of intensive research, experimentation, exploration and teaching of Feng Shui, Master Larry put forth his accumulated knowledge and insights into this book. This book will systematically introduce Feng Shui to its readers. This book is recommended for our Beginning, Intermediate and Advanced Feng Shui classes.

Available in both paperback and ebook. $18.75US

Sang's Luopan

The Luopan is a Chinese compass used in Feng Shui readings. It offers more information for a Feng Shui reading besides the cardinal and inter-cardinal directions. Whereas a Western compass may be used in Feng Shui, a Luopan saves several steps in calculation. The Luopan is 4 inches (10 cm) square. The Luopan is recommended for use in our Feng Shui classes and practice. $50.00US

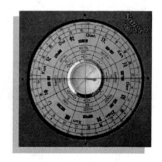

Yi Jing for Love and Marriage

In the journey of life, we often experience times of doubt, confusion and feeling lost. What should we do when facing this type of situation? The Changing Hexagram Divination method can help by prediting what may happen. It can provide guidelines for coping with difficult situations or insight into beneficial ones. This book provides a simple method for the reader to predict the answers to their questions and to help others. Besides resolving confustion and doubt, it also provides a fun hobby for those interested in the ancient art of divination. Use this book as your consultant on Love and Marriage when the need arises!

Available in both paperback and ebook. $14.75US

Ten-Thousand Year Calendar (1882 - 2031)

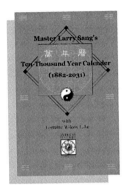

Normally printed in Chinese, but now in English, this handy reference guide is what the Chinese call the Ten-Thousand Year Calendar. This calendar contains information for 150 years, from 1882 to 2031. It gives the annual, monthly, and daily stem and branch, the annual and monthly flying star, as well as the lunar day of the month. It also gives information about the lunar and solar months, the solstices, equinoxes, and the beginning of the four seasons in the Chinese calendar. The Ten-Thousand Year Calendar is used for Feng Shui, Chinese Astrology, Day Selection, and various predictive techniques. 165 Pages.

Available in ebook only. $26.00US

Feng Shui Facts and Myths

This book is a collection of stories about Feng Shui and Astrology. Master Sang attempts to explain aspects of Feng Shui and Chinese Astrology, as the terms are understood or misunderstood in the West. This book will provide you with deeper information on the Chinese cultural traditions of Feng Shui and Astrology.

Available in paperback and ebook. $16.00US

Larry Sang's
2010 Chinese Astrology & Feng Shui Guide
- The Year of the Tiger

Each section explains how to determine the key piece: determining your animal sign; how to read the Feng Shui of your home; and how to read the Day Selection calendar - a valuable day by day indication of favorable and unfavorable activity.

Available in both paperback and ebook. $14.75US

COURSE CATALOG

The following is a current list of the courses available from *The American Feng Shui Institute*. Please consult our online catalog for course fees, descriptions and new additions.

FENG SHUI

CLASS	CLASS NAME	PREREQUISITE
FS095	Introduction to Feng Shui	
FS101/OL	Beginning Feng Shui & Online	-
FS102/OL	Intermediate Feng Shui & Online	-
FS201/OL	Advanced Feng Shui & Online	FS102 or FS101/OL
FS205/OL	Advanced Sitting and Facing & Online	FS101 or FS102/OL
FS106/OL	Additional concepts on Sitting & Facing	FS102/OL
FS225	Feng Shui Folk Beliefs	FS201
FS227/OL	Professional Skills for Feng Shui Consultants	FS201
FS231	Feng Shui Yourself & Your Business	FS201
FS235	Symptoms of a House	FS201
FS250	Explanation of Advanced Feng Shui Theories	FS201
FS275	9 Palace Grid and Pie chart Graph Usage & Online	FS201
FS280	Advanced East West Theory	FS201
FS301	Advanced Feng Shui Case Study 1 & 2	FS201
FS303	Advanced Feng Shui Case Study 3 & 4	FS201
FS305/OL	Advanced Feng Shui Case Study 5 & Online	FS201
FS306/OL	Advanced Feng Shui Case Study 6 & Online	FS201
FS307/OL	Advanced Feng Shui Case Study 7 & Online	FS201
FS308/OL	Advanced Feng Shui Case Study 8 & Online	FS201
FS309	Advanced Feng Shui Case Study 9 & 10	FS201
FS311	Advanced Feng Shui Case Study 11	FS201
FS312/OL	Advanced Feng Shui Case Study 12	FS201
FS313/OL	Advanced Feng Shui Case Study 13 & Online	FS201 & AS101
FS314	Advanced Feng Shui Case Study 14	FS201
FS315	Advanced Feng Shui Case Study 15	FS201
FS316	Advanced Feng Shui Case Study 16 & 17	FS201
FS319	Advanced Feng Shui Case Study 19 & 20	FS201
FS321	Advanced Feng Shui Case Study 20 & 21	FS201
FS340/OL	Secrets of the Five Ghosts	FS201
FS341	The Secrets of the "San Ban Gua"	FS201
FS260/OL	Lawsuit Support & Online	FS201 & AS101

FENG SHUI

FS270/OL	The Taisui, Year Breaker, Three Sha & Online	FS201 & AS101
FS350/OL	Feng Shui Day Selection 1 & Online	FS201 & AS101
FS351/OL	Feng Shui Day Selection 2 & Online	FS201 & FS350/OL
FS360/OL	Marriage and Life Partner Selection Online	FS201 & AS101
FS375/OL	Introduction to Yin House Feng Shui	FS201

YI JING

YJ101	Beginning Yi Jing Divination	AS101
YJ102	Yi Jing Coin Divination	AS101
YJ103	Plum Flower Yi Jing Calculation	AS101

CHINESE ASTROLOGY

AS101	Stems and Branches & Online	-
AS102	Four Pillars 1 & 2 (Zi Ping Ba Zi)	AS101 or AS101/OL
AS103	Four Pillars 3 & 4 (Zi Ping Ba Zi)	AS102
AS105	Four Pillars 5 & 6 (Zi Ping Ba Zi)	AS103
AS201A/OL	Beginning Zi Wei Dou Shu, Part 1	AS101
AS201B/OL	Beginning Zi Wei Dou Shu, Part 2	AS201A/OL
AS211/OL	Intermediate Zi Wei Dou Shu	AS201B/OL
AS301A/OL	Advanced Zi Wei Dou Shu, Part 1	AS211/OL
AS301B/OL	Advanced Zi Wei Dou Shu, Part 2	AS201A/OL
AS311/OL	Zi Wei Dou Shu Case Study 1	AS301B/OL
AS313/OL	Zi Wei Dou Shu Case Study 3	AS301B/OL
AS314	Zi Wei Dou Shu Case Study 2 & 4	AS301B/OL

CHINESE ASTROLOGY

CA101/OL	Palm & Face Reading 1 & 2	-
CA102	Palm & Face Reading 3 & 4	CA101 or CA101/OL
CA103	Palm & Face Reading for Health	-
CA121	Introduction to Chinese Medicine	-
CA110	Professional Face Reading	-

CHINESE ASTROLOGY

CP101	Introduction to Daode Jing	-
CP102	Feng Shui Yourself	-

CLASSES AT THE AMERICAN FENG SHUI INSITUTE:

Due to the limited seating capacity, reservations are necessary and seats are on a first come first serve basis. To reserve your seat, a $50.00 US deposit is required and is non-refundable if cancellation by student takes place less than three days before class. Please mail-in check or call us to reserve your seat with a credit card.* Balance is due on the first day of class.

ONLINE CLASSES WITH THE
AMERICAN FENG SHUI INSTITUTE FEATURE:

- Easy navigation
- Self tests at the end of each module
- A discussion board with trained Institute instructors
- Audio clips for prnounciation
- An online discussion board
- An instant feedback final exam

The online classes are self-paced study modules. They are segmented into four, one-week lessons that lead you at your own pace, over the four-week course. You have 60 days to complete the course work.

For more information, please see our website:
www.amfengshui.com

You may register at any time online, by phone or fax:

Tel: (626) 571-2757
Fax: (626) 281-0042

Email: fsinfo@amfengshui.com

American Feng Shui Institute
111 N. Atlantic Blvd. Suite 352
Monterey Park, CA 91754

*Please **DO NOT** email credit card information at this is not a secure method*

AS A STUDENT OF
THE AMERICAN FENG SHUI INSTITUTE:

You will receive a certificate of completion from the American Feng Shui Institute, for the Beginning/Intermediate and Advanced Feng Shui Classes. Please do not confuse this certification as licensing, as there are no requirements for practitioner at this time.

As a student of the Institute, we are available to assist you with your studies. We have an online Bulletin Board for questions and answers, featuring a topic search. You will obtrain access to the Bulletin Board upon completion of the Advanced Feng Shui class. Due to the complexity of the courses, graduates may repeat in the classroom that you have already taken, for $45.00 US per day, pending available seats. Please see our online course catalog for the most current course offerings.

CANCELLATION AND REFUND POLICY:

All institutional charges shall be returned to the registrant less a $50.00 US cancellation fee, if cancellation notice is received prior to or on the first day of instruction. Any notification of withdrawal or cancellation and any request for a refund are required to be made in writing.

Refunds shall be made within thirty (30) days of receipt of the withdrawal or cancellation notice and refund request.

The institute does not participate in the Student Tuition Recovery Fund (STRF). We are registered with the State of California. Registration means we have met certain minimum standards imposed by the state for registered schools on the basis of our written application to the state. Registration does not mean we have met all of the more extensive standards required by the state for schools that are approved to operate or license or that the state has verified the information we submitted with our registration form.